The
Crystal
Experience

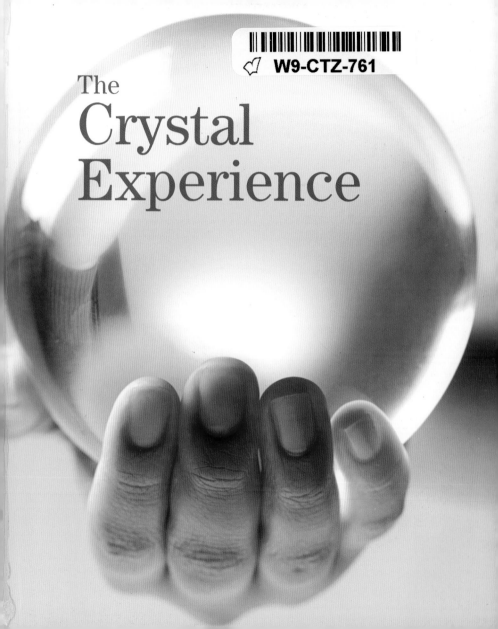

The Crystal Experience

Your complete crystal workshop in a book

Judy Hall

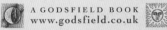

A GODSFIELD BOOK
www.godsfield.co.uk

An Hachette UK Company
www.hachette.co.uk

First published in Great Britain in 2010 by
Godsfield, a division of Octopus Publishing Group Ltd
Endeavour House
189 Shaftesbury Avenue
London
WC2H 8JY
www.octopusbooksusa.com

Distributed in the U.S. and Canada by Octopus Books USA:
c/o Hachette Book Group
237 Park Avenue
New York, NY 10017

ISBN 978-1-84181-392-9

Printed and bound in China

2 4 6 8 10 9 7 5 3 1

Disclaimer
No medical claims are made for the stones in this book and
the information given is not intended to act as a substitute for
medical treatment. If you are in any doubt about their use, a
qualified crystal-healing practitioner should be consulted. In
the context of this book, illness is thought of as a "dis-ease,"
the final manifestation of spiritual, environmental,
psychological, karmic, emotional, or mental imbalance
or distress. Healing means bringing mind, body, and spirit
back into balance and facilitating evolution for the soul, it
does not imply a cure.

In accordance with crystal-healing consensus, all stones are
referred to as crystals, regardless of whether or not they
have a crystalline structure.

CONTENTS

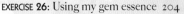

CD tracks

TRACK 1: Relaxation, focusing, and opening the mind's eye

TRACK 2: Attuning to my crystals

TRACK 3: Music only

TRACK 4: The Quartz crystal journey

TRACK 5: The Rainbow Obsidian journey

Introduction

Have you ever wanted to get up close and personal with your crystals? To become totally attuned to them? Have you read a book about crystal properties and thought I'd so like to know more, to really experience this for myself? Well, now you can. My books *The Crystal Bible volume 1* and *volume 2* describe in detail the attributes of almost five hundred crystals and their healing properties. This book is different. Rather than telling you what each crystal does, it helps you to discover for yourself how you respond to a particular crystal and what that crystal has to offer you. It is exactly like attending a workshop with me to explore how you can work with crystals for self-healing and personal development *in the right way for you*.

In my workshops, I don't tell people what to do or what to expect. Instead I encourage them to experience a crystal for themselves by opening their minds to exciting possibilities and playing joyfully with the wondrous little beings that are crystals. I know that everybody is unique and everyone experiences the energy of a particular crystal differently because of personal expectations, past experiences, energetic overlays, emotional blocks, environmental factors, and the effects of spiritual practices.

Some of my most potent crystal remedies have come about through what I call serendipitious synchronicity —the right crystals happened to be there at the right time. In one workshop, for example, a surprisingly large Stibnite wand sat in front of me alongside a huge Chlorite Quartz long point, both recently purchased, plus a beloved piece of Selenite that also formed a wand. When I put these crystals on the table I had no idea what I would use them for. But when I suddenly needed a portal to help lost souls depart this world and go to the light, I picked up the three crystals and held them one on top of the other. This created an extremely efficient portal, and many smaller versions are now in use all over the world. Similarly, I intuitively used Vivianite to heal an extremely sore eye before I intellectually knew that this was

an eye crystal, and a Cathedral Quartz took away a nasty backache just weeks before one of my favorite crystal shop owners said, "I give anyone who comes into the shop with a pain or who feels under the weather one of these to hold and they go out feeling so much better."

So, this book helps you to find out for yourself exactly which crystals resonate with you. It helps you to explore their subtle energies and vibrations, colors and shapes, and it takes you on journeys deep into the heart of yourself and All That Is. You'll find guidance on choosing crystals, building up a crystal collection, and expanding your knowledge, whether you are a beginner or an experienced crystal worker. By taking part in this crystal workshop you will develop your skills in relaxation, visualization, and intuition, too. Relaxation involves entering a receptive state of mind in which your attention is focused inward and disregards external stimuli yet remains alert. Visualization means seeing pictures in your mind's eye and taking journeys through your imagination into other ways of being. When you develop your intuition, you pay attention to the subtle messages that your body, mind, and environment are sending you all the time but that you may not have noticed up to now.

You will find it helpful to relax, focus, and open your mind's eye before undertaking any of the journeys in this book. With practice, this preparation will take only a few moments.

Work with the CD now Play Track 1 of the CD and learn how to relax, focus your intention, and open your mind's eye (to follow the script, see pages 242–43). If you would like to listen to the track lying down, place seven Amethysts around your head to create a calm space and an Apophyllite pyramid over your third eye at the center of your forehead to open your mind's eye.

Throughout this book you will find symbols to guide you into the next stage of your crystal exploration.

This exercise/journey is suitable for Exercises are usually given for a specific crystal, so this symbol tells you which other crystals in your collection you could also use. Journeying with several crystals helps you to establish the differences between them and find exactly the right one for you.

Work with your crystal/s now This symbol guides you to the relevant practical exercise when you are ready, where you will find full instructions to follow.

I'm not quite there yet If you don't yet feel confident about doing the exercise, this symbol gives suggestions for ways to revise and prepare yourself.

Work with the CD now This symbol tells you when you need to turn on the CD and which track to select. The Inspirations chapter on pages 241–49 has some scripts for you to follow.

How to use the book and CD

This book is divided into different sections that have been specially designed to lead you step-by-step into a deeper energetic understanding of crystals as you gain in experience and confidence.

In the first part of each section you will find a brief introduction to the subject, suggestions of which crystals you could use, and directions to guide you to the practical exercises once you feel ready to experience the crystal for yourself. There are also suggestions for what to do if you're not quite ready for the practical experience. At every stage you have the choice to move on or to revise previous work so that you can take things at your own pace and gradually build up your knowledge.

In the second part of each section of the book you will find exercises, guided questions, and space to record your experiences and the answers and insights you have discovered. You can read about the properties of the crystals before you work with a crystal, either in *The Crystal Bible* volumes or in the Crystal Directory on pages 26–32. Alternatively, wait until after you have completed a practical exercise to look up the crystal's properties, or simply work with the qualities you discover for yourself.

The CD that accompanies this book has been devised to guide you into the relaxed, receptive state that best facilitates crystal journeys and experiences. When you play the track recommended for an exercise (as directed by the CD symbol) just follow the instructions you hear. There will be a musical interlude while you carry them out, followed by more instructions guiding you to the next stage of the exercise. If you need further time to practice, pause the CD and move on when you are ready. You will also find a music-only track on the CD to use as an optional background accompaniment to many of the exercises. This lasts for 20 minutes and its ending closes the exercise.

Building up a picture

Recording your insights and experiences is essential if you are to get the most out of this book, and space is provided for you to write your experiences into the book after each exercise. When writing down your observations, remember to record the date and time and the crystal you used. By varying the time you do the exercises, you can find out whether there

is a particular time of day when you are more intuitive or receptive to crystal energies. Some people find it easer to work with crystals in the morning, for instance, and others in the afternoon or evening. If you find there is a significant difference, time your sessions accordingly.

Recording your experiences in the present tense—"I am walking ... I am hearing ..." and so on—helps you to re-enter more fully into the experience later and recall as much information as possible. Write down even the tiniest, seemingly least significant detail, because it may assume greater importance later. Remember to pay attention to the sensations in your body: the feelings you have, the thoughts that pass through your mind, the sounds or smells you become aware of, how your heart rate and breathing change, and, most of all, whether any particular area of your body is affected by the crystal. Part of you might tingle, for example, or become uncomfortable, hot, cold, or painful; alternatively, it might feel comforted or soothed.

The journal entries include questions to help you focus on how the crystal affected you, the emotional, mental, or energetic changes it brought about, and the insights you received about the crystal's properties. Filling these in as fully as possible will help you to monitor your insights and keep track of the ways in which your intuition opens. Don't hesitate to go back and add to the record if you remember something later —but do put the date and time beside it, making it clear that this is an addition to the original record. You might find it helpful to hold the crystal you worked with as you record your insights and then to return to it for several days afterward, sitting quietly and holding the crystal for a few minutes to see if any new insights arise.

Glossary of terms

You will encounter many of these crystal-healing terms as you work through the book; familiarizing yourself with them now will help you to gain more from the exercises.

All That Is

Spirit, the Source, the divine. The sum total of everything that is.

Aura/subtle body

Subtle bio-energetic field surrounding the physical body, which can be sensed intuitively. The aura holds imprints of emotions, blockages, thoughts, and injuries.

Cellular memory

Genetic or past-life information encoded into the cells.

Chakra

Linkage point between subtle energy and the physical body. Chakra malfunction leads to physical, emotional, mental, and spiritual *dis-ease*.

Crystal

All stones, gems, and minerals in their raw state, regardless of whether they have a crystalline structure.

Dis-ease

Final manifestation of spiritual, environmental, psychological, karmic, emotional, or mental imbalance or distress.

Etheric blueprint

Subtle energy pattern, program or grid from which the physical body is constructed. It carries imprints from past lives, previous attitudes, trauma or injury, and ancestral beliefs.

Geopathic stress

Negative energy carried by the earth, generated by water, electromagnetic stress, and other disturbances.

Grids/gridding/layouts

Placing crystals around yourself or a building to bring about balance, energy enhancement, or protection.

Grounding/grounded

Anchoring energies in the earth; being fully connected to your physical body and the earth on which you walk.

Healing

Bringing the body and its subtle energies, mind, spirit, and emotions back into balance on all levels. Healing does not imply cure.

Healing challenge

Some crystals may rapidly release underlying causes of *dis-ease*, temporarily worsening a condition (a catharsis). If this occurs, remove the crystal and rebalance yourself by holding Smoky Quartz or another appropriate crystal.

Higher vibration/resonance

Refined, purer vibration that usually resonates faster. Higher vibrations exist on earth, in the physical body or in other dimensions.

Journeying

When the consciousness leaves day-to-day awareness and travels through various dimensions and locations.

Lightbody

Subtle energy body vibrating at a high frequency. A vehicle for *Spirit*.

Meridians

Subtle energy channels that radiate through the physical body and can be accessed through acupuncture points.

Self

The higher, extended part of you that is not totally incarnated within your physical body and that can therefore access other lives and other dimensions and the totality of your being.

Spirit/Source

See *All That Is*.

Celestite cluster

Onyx ball

HOW DO I CHOOSE A CRYSTAL?

What's in my collection?

It's always handy to keep a selection of crystals ready for use, and the Crystal Directory on pages 26–32 will help you to identify which ones you already have. It will also highlight gaps in your collection.

You can choose either tumbled or raw crystals—and why not have both? Tumbled stones are comfortable to lay on your body, and raw stones can be placed around your environment. You don't have to buy crystals to add to your collection. You can also use crystals that you find in nature, such as Flint, which

has been used in healing for thousands of years, or Snow Quartz pebbles from a beach or river. If you have an aversion to certain crystals or colors, turn to pages 118–19 to find out why.

It is wise to collect a selection of colors and shapes (see pages 54–64) because each one has specific properties and chakra associations (see pages 82–88). However, as you work through the book, you are sure to discover other crystals that resonate with you and your chakras.

 This exercise is suitable for All the crystals in your current collection.

 Work with your crystals now To work out which crystals you have in your collection and what to use them for, turn to Exercise 1: Identifying My Crystals on page 34.

Choosing a crystal

There are three main ways to choose a crystal: rationally, intuitively, and by dowsing. All three selection methods work with any crystal. Crystal energy is subtle, but once you are attuned to it and focused you will quickly be able to recognize the right crystal for you. Don't forget to write down all the crystals you choose on pages 35–39.

Choosing a crystal rationally

The rational way to choose a crystal is to look up the property you are seeking in the Crystal Directory on pages 26–32 or in the indexes to *The Crystal Bible* volumes or *Crystal Prescriptions*. Then go into a shop or online and buy the appropriate crystal. However, once you have bought a range of crystals you still need to choose exactly which one to work with on any occasion. To do this it is useful to open your intuition and listen for the crystal that is calling you, or you could try dowsing.

Choosing a crystal intuitively

Allowing a crystal to "speak" to you involves opening your inner eyes and ears and seeking with your heart rather than your head to find out which crystal would like to be worked with. You can do this at home using your own collection or whenever you're in a crystal shop. First, relax and quieten your mind, then choose the crystal that your eyes first alight on, the one that seems to stick to your fingers or the one you suddenly realize you've been carrying around the shop. When you connect with the crystal's vibration, you may feel your energy jump or tingle—like getting an electric shock—or slow and deepen. It may pulse in your hand or you may actually hear the crystal's note.

 This exercise is suitable for Any crystal in your collection or a crystal shop.

 Work with your crystals now To explore finger dowsing further, turn to Exercise 2: What Do My Fingers Tell Me? on page 40.

Choosing a crystal by finger dowsing

This is an excellent way to choose a crystal. It harnesses your body's innate ability to tell you what is good for you and what is not.

Begin by looping your thumb and finger together as shown. (Use whichever hand instinctively feels right to you.)

Slip your other thumb and finger through the loop and close them. Hold the loop over a crystal and ask if this one is beneficial for you.

Pull steadily. If the loop breaks, the answer is no. If the loop holds, the answer is yes. Remember to record your results on pages 35–39.

Cleansing, activating, and storing crystals

Many people ask why crystals don't work for them and why they feel dragged down rather than uplifted when they handle a crystal. Frequently, this is because the crystal hasn't yet been asked to work or been attuned to the user's unique energy frequency. An even more likely answer is that it hasn't been cleansed before use. Crystals pick up vibrations from everyone who handles them, and they also absorb negative energies. So, if you don't cleanse your crystals you'll pick up bad vibes and won't feel the benefits that a purified crystal can bring you.

Cleansing crystals

You can cleanse and recharge most crystals by holding them under running water for a few minutes and then placing them in the sun for a few hours. Natural water, such as a stream or the sea, is best (put small crystals in a bag to prevent them from being washed away), although you can use tap water. If there is no sun available, visualize bright white light radiating down onto the crystals. It is best to cleanse fragile, layered, or friable crystals by placing them in brown rice overnight. They can also be laid on a large Quartz cluster or a Carnelian. White stones enjoy recharging in moonlight. Always cleanse your crystals before and after you use them for healing.

Activating crystals

Close your eyes and concentrate on the crystals. See them surrounded by bright white light. Ask that they be attuned to your own unique frequency and that they be activated to act for your highest good. Ask for the crystals to be blessed by the highest energies in the universe and for them to be dedicated to your own self-healing and the healing of the environment around you.

Storing crystals

A cloth bag is a good place to store tumbled stones, but more delicate stones can be kept wrapped in a cloth or displayed on a shelf. Be aware that crystals that are worn or kept in your environment absorb negative energies and need regular cleansing.

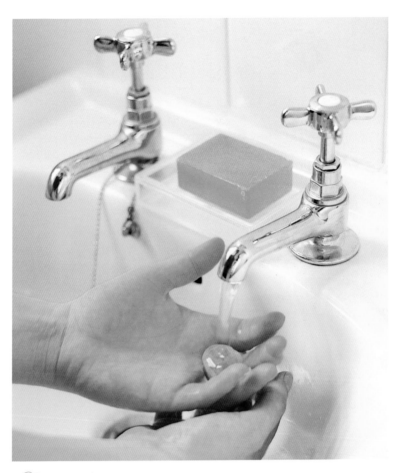

 **This exercise is suitable for** Cleansing is essential for all crystals.

Work with your crystals now To carry out a thorough crystal cleanse and activation, turn to Exercise 3: The Big Crystal Cleanse on pages 42–43.

Which crystals will I need?

I have chosen the crystals in the Crystal Directory on pages 26–32 carefully to cover a wide spectrum of colors and properties and because they are relatively cheap and easy to track down. These make a good collection to begin with. However, do add your own personal favorite crystals to this list; the directory is not intended to be definitive. Once you have assembled and cleansed your crystals (see pages 22–23), you can begin the practical exercises.

As you become more experienced, you might like to work with higher vibration crystals, and these are profiled in a separate directory on pages 212–17. Again, you may attract more of these amazing consciousness-raising beauties to yourself than are profiled on those pages. You need to check out the properties of high-vibration crystals carefully because they tend to be specifically attuned to certain frequencies or vibrations that must mesh with your own energetic emanations. If you don't connect with one crystal, try another and return to the first one later.

 This exercise is suitable for Any crystal in your collection.

 Work with your crystal now To prepare yourself to spend time with a crystal, turn to Exercise 4: Attuning to My Crystals on page 44.

 I'm not quite there yet If you haven't yet learned to cleanse or activate a crystal, turn back to pages 22–23.

CRYSTAL DIRECTORY

Bloodstone (trigonal; red and green)
An excellent all-round healer, Bloodstone stimulates or sedates the immune system as required and has been used for thousands of years to heal the kidneys and blood. Instills courage and selflessness and helps you to act in the present moment.

Halite (cubic; pink, white, or blue)
A useful physical and emotional cleanser, Halite assists in spiritual purification and detachment. It brings about metabolic and cellular balance and, ameliorating water retention, is helpful for skin conditions and detoxification. Overcomes anger, abandonment, and rejection and instills contentment. Dissolves in water.

Rose Quartz (trigonal; pink)
A crystal of unconditional love and forgiveness, Rose Quartz calms and gently dissolves negativity or grief. The perfect emotional healer, it brings about necessary change and is also excellent for the circulatory and respiratory systems. Instills compassion and empathy and overcomes deprivation.

Garnet (cubic; red, green, orange)
A powerful energizing and regeneration crystal, especially for the chakras, metabolism, and libido, Garnet is a sexual stimulant, removing inhibitions. It can also be used for purification and healing the blood and circulation. Releases anger and strengthens the survival instinct.

Halite

Rose Quartz

Bloodstone

Garnet

Jasper (trigonal; all colors) Available in a multitude of colors, patterns, and forms, Jasper sustains during time of stress and induces tranquility. It aligns the chakras and facilitates journeying. Traditionally used for protection and to support the circulatory system and the digestive and sexual organs. Encourages assertiveness, organizational skills, and self-honesty.

Carnelian (trigonal; red, pink, and orange) A crystal of prosperity and vitality, Carnelian helps you to be fully present. A useful protector, especially against other people's rage, it has traditionally been used to support the reproductive organs and circulatory system and to increase fertility. Instills courage, enhances analytic skills, and helps you to overcome abuse.

Amber (amorphous; yellowish brown, green) An ancient crystal of healing and protection, Amber is a powerful cleanser and regenerator. It can lift depression and is a useful mental enlivener; it also promotes emotional trust and encourages the body to heal itself. Enhances self-expression and decision-making.

Citrine (trigonal; yellow, smoky) An exceptional attractor of abundance, Citrine also acts as a powerful cleanser and invigorator. This crystal enhances self-esteem and confidence and promotes joy. Excellent for concentration. Enhances creativity and generosity of spirit.

Carnelian

Amber

Blue Jasper

Citrine

Calcite (hexagonal; all colors) A useful purifier, Calcite amplifies energy and alleviates stress. Available in most colors, it promotes emotional intelligence and hopefulness and increases motivation, helping to combat laziness. Instills discernment and serenity.

Aventurine (trigonal; green, blue, peach) Exceptionally useful for blocking geopathic stress and electromagnetic smog, Green Aventurine prevents psychic vampires from pulling on your energy. Aventurine has traditionally been used to attract prosperity and helps you to see alternative possibilities. Instills compassion and leadership qualities and calms anger.

Moss Agate (trigonal; green and blue) A crystal of great stability that encourages fertility, Moss Agate is an excellent all-round energy protector and environmental enhancer. A crystal of new beginnings that strengthens positive personality traits, it has traditionally been used to assist birth. Helps intellectual people to access their feelings and emotional people to gain objectivity.

Malachite (monoclinic; green) Bringing issues and negativity to the surface rapidly, Malachite absorbs environmental and emotional toxins. A crystal of transformation, it assists in inner journeys and mercilessly pinpoints anything blocking spiritual growth. The intensity of Malachite goes to the core of a problem and accesses your shadow. Encourages risk-taking and releases outworn patterns.

Aventurine

Moss Agate

Calcite

Malachite

Peridot (orthorhombic; green)
A protective crystal for the aura, Peridot was traditionally believed to repel evil spirits. It is useful for removing old baggage or obsessions and releasing guilt, jealousy, and stress. Instills emotional clarity and shows how to forgive yourself.

Jade (monoclinic; all colors) One of the ancient stones of prosperity and protection, Jade imbues the soul with serenity. It has traditionally been used to heal the kidneys and balance fluids in the body. Inspires dreams, stimulates ideas, and instills self-sufficiency.

Chrysocolla (monoclinic/orthorhombic; blue-green) A tranquil crystal, Chrysocolla assists in both meditation and spiritual communication.

It helps you to accept with serenity situations that cannot be changed and to keep silent when appropriate. It enhances self-awareness and confidence, promoting truthfulness and a cool head.

Turquoise (triclinic; blue-green)
Highly prized since ancient times as an excellent healer and protector, Turquoise consoles the soul. Useful for problem-solving, it promotes self-realization and alleviates feelings of martyrdom or self-sabotage. Useful for strengthening the meridians and alleviating cramps and pain.

Jade

Chrysocolla

Peridot

Turquoise

Blue Lace Agate (trigonal; blue)
A great throat, thyroid, and eye healer, Blue Lace Agate is calming and nurturing, bringing about inner peace. Transmuting anger, infection, and inflammation, it helps you to express thoughts clearly and to stop suppressing feelings. All Agates enhance mental function, ameliorate confusion, and overcome bitterness of the heart.

Kyanite (triclinic; blue, black)
The striations of tranquilizing Kyanite powerfully transmit and attract energy. Useful for dream-recall and transitions of any kind, Kyanite cleanses the meridians and energy lines and cuts through pretence. Dispels illusions and frustration and increases the capacity for logical, linear thought.

Lapis Lazuli (cubic; blue with gold)
Helpful for the throat and third eye, Lapis Lazuli heals problems associated with not speaking out. Harmonizing all the levels of being, it helps you to access your purpose in life. Lets you take charge of your life and brings deep self-knowledge.

Sugilite (hexagonal; purple)
One of the major love stones, Sugilite shows how to live your truth. Useful for healing dyslexia and trauma, it is particularly helpful for misfits. Sugilite helps you to overcome shock, upsets, and disappointment. A useful crystal for groups, it dissipates hostility and instills forgiveness. Helps you to face up to and alleviate unpleasant emotional truths.

Kyanite

Lapis Lazuli

Blue Lace Agate

Sugilite

Amethyst (trigonal; purple) A highly protective crystal, Amethyst acts as a natural tranquilizer, balancing emotional highs and lows and counteracting geopathic stress. Useful for boosting hormones, it helps neural signals to pass through the brain. Facilitates decision-making and helps you feel less scattered, and in setting realistic goals.

Fluorite (cubic; most colors) A useful viral healer, Fluorite is traditionally used to strengthen bones and teeth. Preventing dis-ease from electromagnetic stress, it dissolves fixed patterns. Fluorite helps you to discern when outside influences are affecting your behavior. It also works to dissolve fixed ideas so that you see the bigger picture. Removes illusion and reveals truth.

Quartz (trigonal; white) One of the most energetic stones on the planet and a master healer, Quartz generates, conserves, amplifies, or releases energy, as required. In its many forms, it works at the level appropriate to you. A natural storehouse of information, it assists concentration. Different varieties offer a wide spectrum of qualities.

Apophyllite (tetragonal; white) An excellent activator of intuition and spiritual vision, Apophyllite is a powerful vibrational transmitter. It promotes introspection and insight into causes of behavior and any dis-ease you may have and is useful for Reiki. Alleviating apprehension, it allows you to tolerate uncertainty and make decisions from your spirit rather than your ego. Helps to overcome anxiety.

Purple Fluorite

Quartz

Amethyst

Apophyllite

Hematite (trigonal; red, silver when polished) One of the most useful grounding stones, Hematite harmonizes body, mind, and spirit. Strongly yang, it balances the meridians, focuses concentration, and supports when you feel vulnerable. Excellent for imparting confidence and also for enhancing willpower.

Smoky Quartz (trigonal; brown-gray) An excellent grounding and detoxifying crystal, Smoky Quartz is useful for protection especially against geopathic stress. It relieves depression and assists you in accepting your physical body,

enhancing virility and potency. This crystal helps you to feel more comfortable in your body and in manifesting your dreams. Promotes positive, pragmatic thought.

Tourmaline (trigonal; most colors) An excellent crystal against psychic attack, Black Tourmaline also protects against geopathic stress or environmental unrest. Other colors offer a wide range of healing options, especially for overcoming emotional dysfunction. Helps you to find solutions to specific problems and assists you in understanding yourself and others.

Smoky Quartz

Hematite

Green Tourmaline

CHOOSING AND CLEANSING EXERCISES

The exercises on the following pages will help you get to know your crystals and their properties and qualities. You will also learn how to keep them at their sparkling, energetic best and how to open your crystal intuition. Remember to record your experiences in the spaces provided in each exercise.

What's in my collection?

This exercise helps you to work out exactly which crystals you have in your collection and what you can use them for. It also allows you to keep track of the additional discoveries you make as you explore your crystals in later activities in the book. Remember to date all entries.

Exercise 1 IDENTIFYING MY CRYSTALS

- Using either the Crystal Directory on pages 26–32 or *The Crystal Bible* volume 1 or volume 2, identify each crystal in your collection and list it in the fill-in spaces between pages 35 and 39.

- Write down the crystal's known properties and any effects you have noticed when holding or working with it. There is space to fill in new discoveries as you work through the book.

- Date the entry so that you can track your increasing knowledge and insight.

- As you add new crystals to your collection, be sure to list them and also list any different colors or forms of basic crystals, such as Jasper or Quartz.

My crystal collection

Crystal _____

Date first worked with _____   Time _____

Properties/effects _____

_____

Additional discoveries _____

_____

_____   Date _____

Crystal _____

Date first worked with _____   Time _____

Properties/effects _____

_____

Additional discoveries _____

_____

_____   Date _____

Crystal _____

Date first worked with _____   Time _____

Properties/effects _____

_____

Additional discoveries _____

_____

_____   Date _____

Crystal _____

Date first worked with _____ Time _____

Properties/effects _____

_____

Additional discoveries _____

_____

_____ Date _____

Crystal _____

Date first worked with _____ Time _____

Properties/effects _____

_____

Additional discoveries _____

_____

_____ Date _____

Crystal _____

Date first worked with _____ Time _____

Properties/effects _____

_____

Additional discoveries _____

_____

_____ Date _____

Crystal _____

Date first worked with _____ Time _____

Properties/effects _____

_____

Additional discoveries _____

_____

_____ Date _____

Crystal _____

Date first worked with _____ Time _____

Properties/effects _____

_____

Additional discoveries _____

_____

_____ Date _____

Crystal _____

Date first worked with _____ Time _____

Properties/effects _____

_____

Additional discoveries _____

_____

_____ Date _____

Crystal _____

Date first worked with _____ Time _____

Properties/effects _____

_____

Additional discoveries _____

_____

_____ Date _____

Crystal _____

Date first worked with _____ Time _____

Properties/effects _____

_____

Additional discoveries _____

_____

_____ Date _____

Crystal _____

Date first worked with _____ Time _____

Properties/effects _____

_____

Additional discoveries _____

_____

_____ Date _____

Crystal _____

Date first worked with _____ Time _____

Properties/effects _____

_____

Additional discoveries _____

_____

_____ Date _____

Crystal _____

Date first worked with _____ Time _____

Properties/effects _____

_____

_____

Additional discoveries _____

_____ Date _____

Crystal _____

Date first worked with _____ Time _____

Properties/effects _____

_____

Additional discoveries _____

_____

_____ Date _____

Using my intuition

This exercise helps you to become aware of which crystals are calling to you or would like to work with you. If you already dowse using a pendulum, use that method or, for a change, explore this finger-dowsing technique.

Exercise 2 WHAT DO MY FINGERS TELL ME?
CD REFERENCE TRACK 3 (OPTIONAL)

- **You will need** a selection of crystals (already cleansed, see pages 22–23)

- **Placing your finger on one crystal** at a time ask, "Is this the most appropriate and beneficial crystal to work with at this time?" If you have a specific goal, state what it is as you ask the question.

- **Loop one thumb and finger together** as shown on page 21, then loop the thumb and finger of the other hand through and pull. If the loop holds, the answer is yes. If the loop does not hold, select another crystal and repeat the process.

- **Make a record of the crystals** that responded positively to your question and your specific goal, if you had one.

- **To extend this exercise**, go into a crystal shop and finger dowse until you find the crystals that are beneficial for you once cleansed. You could also plunge your hand into a tub of tumbled crystal and see which ones "stick" to your fingers. Now record your experiences in the space provided.

What my fingers told me

Crystal _____

Date _____ Time _____

Goal _____
_____

Result _____
_____

Crystal _____

Date _____ Time _____

Goal _____
_____

Result _____
_____

Crystal _____

Date _____ Time _____

Goal _____
_____

Result _____
_____

Cleansing and activating

Carry out this exercise before using the crystals in your collection for the first time and repeat it whenever you add a new crystal or work on one of the exercises. It is especially important to cleanse your crystals after healing work.

Exercise 3 THE BIG CRYSTAL CLEANSE

- **You will need** crystals from your collection, a tub of uncooked brown rice, running water, a net bag, a cloth for drying

- **On a sunny day gather together** all your crystals. Sort them into two piles: robust tumbled, shaped, or raw stones; and delicate layered crystals, clusters, and those that may dissolve in water.

- **Place the delicate stones** in the tub of rice and leave for several hours (or overnight). As you do so, ask that the crystals be cleansed and purified.

- **If possible carry the more robust crystals** to a natural place where water runs freely or use spring water. Either place the crystals in the water directly or place them in the net bag first if there is a danger of them being washed away. As you do so, ask that the crystals be cleansed and purified.

- **Carefully dry the wet crystals** and place them in the sun for as long as possible to revitalize and recharge them (white stones like to be placed outside beneath the light of the moon, too). If possible, place the crystals directly onto the earth or a rock during this recharging period.

- **Hold the cleansed crystals in your hands**, or place your hands over the crystals if they are too large to hold. Picture them surrounded by bright white light and ask that the crystals work for your highest good and the highest good of anyone who has contact with them.

- **Wait a moment while the crystals adjust** to your unique resonance and come into harmony with your energy.

- **If you have a specific task for the crystals,** such as healing or protection, ask for that now, but do not limit your request; always add "or something better," and/or "anything else that the crystal wishes to offer me."

My crystal cleanse experience

Date _____ Time _____

Crystals _____

My experience _____

_____

Did I notice a difference in the crystals after they had been cleansed? _____

_____

Did I notice a difference after they had been activated? _____

_____

Did it become obvious that the crystal could help me in a specific way? _____

_____

Crystal attunement

This exercise helps you to attune your own vibrations to those of a crystal so that you become more sensitive to crystal energies. You can use the CD track to get to know any crystal in your collection and experience its energy; just work with one cleansed and activated crystal (see pages 22–23) in turn. The CD talks you into a relaxed state, attunes you to the crystal, allows meditation time with the crystal, and then brings you out of the meditation. After each attunement, jot down any sensations you notice in your body, thoughts that come to mind, or emotions you experience. Remember to add any new properties you discover to the crystal's entry on pages 34–39.

 ## Exercise 4 ATTUNING TO MY CRYSTALS

CD REFERENCE TRACK 2

TO FOLLOW THE SCRIPT TURN TO PAGES 244–245

- **You will need**: any cleansed and activated crystal from your collection

- **Sit quietly holding** your crystal. Breathe gently and allow yourself to relax and focus your attention on the crystal. State your intention to get to know this crystal a little better and to feel its energy.

- **Allow your eyes to go into soft focus** and gaze at the crystal. Note its shape, its color and size. Follow its contours and craters, if it has a "window" look inside. Feel how light or heavy the crystal is in your hand. Sense its vibrations and energetic resonance. You may feel your energy jump or tingle—like getting an electric shock—or slow and pulse as it connects to the crystal's energy. Allow the energy of the crystal to travel up your arms and into your heart and mind so that it reveals itself to you.

- **Notice whether the crystal makes a special contact** with any part of your body. If you wish, guide the energy up through your chakras (see pages 82–83) and watch for an energetic response.

- **If the crystal is transparent or translucent**, allow your gaze to pass through the outer edge and into the center; follow the planes and landscape you find there. Crystal energy is subtle, so allow yourself time to attune to the vibrations.

- **When you are ready, put your crystal down** and consciously break contact with its energies. Open your eyes fully and bring your attention into the room. Take your focus to your feet and feel the contact they make with the floor. Feel the contact your sit bones make with the chair; feel them supporting the weight of your body. Picture a bubble of protection all around you. When you feel ready, stand up and move around, then record your insights in the space provided.

Note: Try using both your left and right hands separately to feel the energy as one hand may be more receptive then the other. If so, use this hand in future exercises.

My crystal attunement experience

Crystal _____

Date _____ Time _____

My experience _____
_____
_____

My body sensations _____
_____

My receptive hand _____

My chakra connections _____
_____
_____

My thoughts _____
_____
_____

My emotions _____
_____
_____

My intuitive understanding of what the crystal is offering me _____
_____
_____

My crystal attunement experience

Crystal _____

Date _____ **Time** _____

My experience _____
_____
_____

My body sensations _____
_____
_____

My chakra connections _____
_____
_____

My thoughts _____
_____
_____

My emotions _____
_____
_____

My intuitive understanding of what the crystal is offering me _____
_____
_____

My crystal attunement experience

Crystal _____

Date _____ Time _____

My experience _____
_____
_____

My body sensations _____
_____
_____

My chakra connections _____
_____
_____

My thoughts _____
_____
_____

My emotions _____
_____
_____

My intuitive understanding of what the crystal is offering me _____
_____
_____

ALL ABOUT CRYSTALS

What is a crystal?

Most people think of sparkling gemstones when they hear the word "crystal," but strictly speaking, a crystal is defined as having an orderly, identifiable repeating lattice or internal structure. For the purposes of crystal healing, all kinds of stones—including Flint, meteorites, and solidified resins such as Amber—are referred to as crystals, regardless of whether they are gemstones, semiprecious stones, pieces of rock, or amorphous substances.

How do crystals work?

The blunt answer to this question is that no one knows exactly! People talk about color resonances between crystals and the chakras (see pages 88–89), about the effects of light and energy on our bodies, and the fact that our bodies contain a huge volume of water through which vibrations can pass. But quite why they work as they do is something that we may have to leave to quantum science to explain—which suggests that waves and particles are the same and can be in two places at once. What we do know, however, is that although they may look calm on the outside, internally crystals form a seething mass of energy as their tiny particles vibrate around atomic cores. Whatever else crystals do, they most certainly emit and absorb energies, and this energy can be measured—and experienced.

Ancient peoples believed that everything on and in the earth and the sky was a manifestation of the divine and that crystals were the flesh of the gods. As such, they could be used to attract the benevolent attentions—or deflect the malevolent intentions—of the gods. People believed in the concept of "as above, so below" and of correspondences and similarities. This theory suggests that there is a resonating order throughout the universe and that any part can be used to bring about harmony in the whole, especially where there is a resemblance between the two parts.

Although it arrived on the planet from outer space and does not have a crystalline structure, Moldavite is nevertheless deemed to be a crystal.

Magnesite's similarity to bone caused ancient people to use it for skeletal healing and tooth problems.

Zincite's resemblance to urine crystals prompted a modern crystal healer to suggest its use for urinary infections.

 This exercise is suitable for Any crystal or rock.

 Work with your crystals now To experience the energies of very different crystals, turn to Exercise 5: Feel Me on page 66.

I'm not quite there yet Play track 1 of the CD until you can relax and focus your mind on quietly attuning to the crystal energy.

Do shape and color matter?

Indeed they do! Both the color and the shape of a crystal can affect how its energy flows and the healing work it can do, and attuning yourself to specific colors and shapes expands your knowledge of the ways in which crystals want to work with you. Both color and shape can be artificially amended, which affects how the underlying energies manifest.

Crystal colors

Within their main form, many crystals can be found in a variety of colors. Color arises from the minerals and impurities incorporated when the crystal is created or superheated, although some are artificially dyed or heat-amended to produce a different color—for example Amethyst or Smoky Quartz are heated to form Citrine or Prasiolite, and Mohave Turquoise is dyed deep purple. As a general guide, the following colors have specific effects or properties. However, do not let this limit what an individual crystal can do for you.

Crystal shapes

The internal lattice of a crystal defines the system to which it belongs and affects how energy moves through the crystal. This internal lattice and its precise replication of facets and angles remains the same no matter how the crystal is shaped on the outside—which is why a crystal can be raw or faceted,

 These exercises are suitable for All colors and shapes of crystal.

 Work with your crystals now Select the crystal colors or shapes you wish to experience and then turn to Exercise 6: Which Color Am I? on page 70 or Exercise 3: What Shape Am I? on page 74.

 I'm not quite there yet Study the crystal shapes in your collection and compare them with those on pages 58–61 so that you can quickly identify the different forms.

flawless or chipped and still have the same healing effect. A few crystals that formed rapidly, such as Obsidian, and the resin Amber do not have an internal lattice (see pages 63–64). Regardless of the structure of the internal lattice, the flow of crystal energy is also mediated by the way in which a crystal is shaped externally, whether naturally or by cutting and polishing (see pages 58–61). If you are a beginner, it is easier to start experiencing energy flow by working with shaped crystals before moving on to use the more subtle internal lattice of crystal systems (see pages 63–64).

Crystal variations

Although these stones below and on page 55 all look very different, they are all classified as crystals by crystal enthusiasts. Some crystals are artificially shaped to look different and for specific purposes.

Shaped Crystal Wand

Quartz Cluster

Polished Chalcopyrite

Red Chalcedony Geode

Polished Flint

Raw Pyrophyllite

Raw Cavansite

Amber

Faceted Emerald

Crystalline Hemimorphite

Polished Preseli
Bluestone

Natural Pumice

Polished
Rhodocrosite

Polished Malachite

Tumbled Lapis
Lazuli

Raw Amazonite

Natural Spirit Quartz

Raw Yellow Calcite

Polished Fluorite

DIRECTORY OF COLORS

Rose Quartz

Pink crystals Offering unconditional love, nurturing, and comfort, these crystals are excellent for healing the heart, releasing grief, calming emotions, and instilling acceptance. Ideal for long-term use.

Faceted Ruby

Red crystals Stimulating and strengthening, these crystals are superb for activating creativity and revitalizing potency, but may over-excite volatile emotions. They are traditionally used for alleviating hemorrhages and inflammation. Best for short-term use.

Carnelian

Orange crystals Activating and releasing, these crystals are useful for building up energetic structures. Many attract abundance and stimulate creativity.

Yellow crystals Awakening and organizing, these crystals are particularly active at the mental level and the solar plexus. They calm the emotions and infections. Useful for overcoming seasonal disorders.

Citrine

Green crystals Calming and balancing, these crystals provide healing for the eyes and heart. They are useful when energy needs sedating or emotions need pacifying. Traditionally used for diseases of the eye.

Malachite

Blue crystals Calming and facilitating clear communication and self-expression. These crystals can ground or project spiritual energy. Assist intuition and channeling.

Angelite

Fluorite

Purple, indigo, and lilac crystals
Integrating and aligning, these crystals
have powerful spiritual-awakening
qualities, stimulating service to others.
Useful for cooling over-heated energies.

Snow Quartz

White or clear crystals Purifing and
focusing energy, these crystals link to
the highest realms of being. Excellent
when situations need clarifying or for
opening intuition and gaining insight.

Tiger's Eye

Gray, brown, or black crystals Good
for grounding the physical body and
detoxifying negative energies, these
crystals are useful protectors.
Helpful in grids.

DIRECTORY OF SHAPES

Ball Emits energy equally all round.
Forms a window to move through time.

Quartz ball

Cluster Several points on a base radiate
energy in several directions.

Quartz cluster

Double terminated Points at both ends
emit energy. Breaks old patterns.

Double-terminated Quartz wand

Zoisite egg

Egg The gently pointed end focuses energy.

Elestial

Elestial Gently folded crystal with many terminations, windows, and inner planes. Radiates a gently flowing energy that opens the way to insight and change.

Quartz generator point

Generator Features a six-pointed end or several points radiating equally in all directions. Focuses healing energy or intention and draws people together.

Geode Hollow cave-like formation that amplifies, conserves, and slowly releases energy.

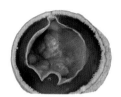

Avalonite geode

Phantom Features a pointed inner pyramid. Breaks old patterns and raises vibrations.

Quartz phantom

Point Draws off energy when pointed out from the body, draws energy in when pointed toward the body. Useful for cleansing and energizing.

Amethyst point

Square Consolidates energy and useful for anchoring intention and grounding. Naturally occurring square crystals, such as Fluorite, draw off negative energy and transform it.

Natural Fluorite square

Quartz scepter

Scepter Crystal formed around a central core rod. An excellent power and restructuring tool.

Tumbled Amphibole

Tumbled Gently rounded stones. Useful in grids or to wear to draw off negative energy or bring in positive vibrations.

Twin

Twin Two crystals of equal length sharing a base. Draws people together.

Natural Quartz wand

Wand Long pointed or specially shaped crystals. Either focus and draw off energy or bring in energy according to which way the point is facing. Useful for joining crystals in a grid.

Crystal systems

Geologists and gemologists assign crystals to seven main groups according to their inner geometric lattice: cubic, hexagonal, monoclinic, orthorhombic, tetragonal, triclinic, and trigonal. There is one further category of crystal, amorphous, which has no lattice because of the speed at which it formed. Each of these groups of crystal is built from a basic shape, but this does not necessarily affect the outer appearance of the crystal. Crystals from these groups are used in advanced healing techniques.

 → **This exercise is suitable for** Crystals from each of the eight systems.

 Work with your crystals now To explore crystal systems, turn to Exercise 8: What System Do I Belong To? on page 78.

Note This exercise is for advanced practitioners who can identify the system to which a crystal belongs and understand energy utilization.

 I'm not quite there yet If you don't know to which system your crystal belongs, check in the Crystal Directory on pages 26–32 or in other reference books. If you don't feel ready for advanced work, spend more time exploring how energy moves through external crystal shapes (see pages 58–61), or turn to the next chapter on page 81 or move onto the other exercises.

DIRECTORY OF GROUPS

Almandine Garnet

Cubic (lattice created from squares with axes at right angles to each other; e.g. Garnet) Stabilizes, grounds, cleanses, releases tension, and encourages creativity.

Faceted Emerald

Hexagonal (lattice created from three-dimensional hexagrams; e.g. Emerald) Organizes and balances energy and provides support; useful for exploring specific issues.

Polished Selenite

Monoclinic (lattice created from parallelograms; e.g. Selenite) Increases perception and balances the body systems; excellent for purification.

Danburite

Orthorhombic (lattice created from rhomboids; e.g. Danburite) Useful cleanser and clearer; increases the flow of information.

Tetragonal (lattice created from rectangles with long and short axes at right angles to each other; e.g. Apophyllite) Transforms, opens, harmonizes, and balances energy flow; brings resolution.

Natural Apophyllite pyramid

Triclinic (lattice formed from trapeziums; e.g. Labradorite) Protects and opens perception, facilitating exploration of other dimensions.

Labradorite

Trigonal (lattice created from triangles; e.g. Tourmaline) Focuses and anchors energy; invigorates and protects the aura.

Tourmaline

Amorphous (no lattice; e.g. Obsidian) Energy flows and acts rapidly; can be a catalyst for growth or catharsis.

Obsidian

SHAPE AND COLOR EXERCISES

The following exercises will help you to understand crystal energies and shapes and to intuitively feel the effect they have on you and your environment. Crystal energies are subtle and may not be experienced in quite the way you expect. Watch out for sensations, either on the surface of your skin or deep within your body, or for feelings out in the aura or around your head or feet. Crystals have their own way of communicating with you, so just relax, be patient and wait for them to make their energy known. The more you can become one with the crystal, the more conscious you will be of the energy to which you are attuning.

Feeling crystal energies

Some people are immediately aware of crystal energies, describing them as "buzzing," "jumping," or "stimulating," or "soothing" and "a stream of energy." Other people find that their moods or mind are more subtly affected. But by practicing this exercise, anyone can learn to sense crystal energies in one way or another and to differentiate between the different shapes.

Exercise 5 FEEL ME
CD REFERENCE TRACK 2 (TO FOLLOW THE SCRIPT, TURN TO PAGES 244–45)

- **You will need** 4 or 5 cleansed and activated crystals or stones of various shapes and/or colors, such as a piece of Flint, some Amber, a gemstone, a rough semiprecious crystal, such as Lapis Lazuli, and a piece of Quartz

- **Relax and place your hand** over each of the crystals in turn and wait to see if you can feel its energy. If you can, record your findings in the spaces provided. If you can't yet sense the energy, play Track 2 of the CD, or change hands.

- **As you follow the instructions** on the CD and allow yourself to relax, open your mind's eye and focus your attention gently on the crystal you are holding. Feel its shape and weight and become one with the crystal and the energies it is resonating. Does it feel fast or slow, hot or cold?

- **When you have experienced the energy** of one crystal, pick up another very different type and repeat the process, noticing the differences.

- **Finally, put all the crystals down** on a table, mix them around and, with your eyes closed, try to identify which crystal is which from its energetic feel. Now record your experiences in the space provided.

My crystal energy experience

Date _____ **Time** _____

Crystal 1 _____

Shape _____ **Color** _____

How did the crystal energy feel? _____
_____
_____

How did it affect me? _____
_____
_____

Did it affect a specific part of my body? _____
_____
_____

Did it change my mood? _____
_____
_____

Did it bring up a particular emotion or thought? _____
_____
_____

Crystal 2 _____

Shape _____ **Color** _____

How did the crystal energy feel? _____

_____

How did it affect me? _____

_____

Did it affect a specific part of my body? _____

Did it change my mood? _____

Did it bring up a particular emotion or thought? _____

How was it different from the first crystal? _____

Crystal 3 _____

Shape _____ **Color** _____

How did the crystal energy feel? _____

_____

How did it affect me? _____

_____

Did it affect a specific part of my body? _____

Did it change my mood? _____

Did it bring up a particular emotion or thought? _____

How was it different from the other crystals? _____

Crystal 4 _____

Shape _____ **Color** _____

How did the crystal energy feel? _____

_____

How did it affect me? _____

_____

Did it affect a specific part of my body? _____

Did it change my mood? _____

Did it bring up a particular emotion or thought? _____

How was it different from the first crystal? _____

Crystal 5 _____

Shape _____ **Color** _____

How did the crystal energy feel? _____

_____

How did it affect me? _____

_____

Did it affect a specific part of my body? _____

Did it change my mood? _____

Did it bring up a particular emotion or thought? _____

How was it different from the other crystals? _____

Experiencing color

This exercise helps you to understand the effect color brings to a specific crystal and to identify which ones work best for you. You can also use this exercise to work with different colors of crystal generally rather than comparing those of one type only. Remember to use your receptive hand.

Exercise 6 WHICH COLOR AM I?
CD REFERENCE TRACK 3 (OPTIONAL)

- **You will need:** cleansed and activated crystals, such as Jasper or Quartz, in as many different colors as possible, a table, a white cloth

- **Pick one color of the crystal** and hold it quietly for a few moments. Notice whether it feels hot or cold, lively or calming, and any immediate effect it has on you at the physical, emotional, mental, auric, or spiritual level. Particularly note if you are especially attracted or repulsed by the crystal (you can work with this later, see pages 118–19).

- **Hold the crystal at a distance** from your body, then bring it close to you and see how it feels. Does its energy get stronger? Does your body respond? Does your mood or thought-pattern change?

- **Beginning at the top of your head,** slowly pass the crystal down the midline of your body and notice any sensations you feel.

- **Stop at each chakra (see pages 82–83)** and check the effect, if any, that a particular color of crystal has on that chakra.

- **Repeat with another color.** When you have worked with each of the colors, put all the crystals on a table on a neutral base, such as a white cloth. Close your eyes and swirl the crystals around several times.

- **Keeping your eyes closed,** pick up each crystal in turn and try to name the color. Write down your thoughts in the space provided.

- **Repeat the exercise at a different** time of day and practice until you can correctly identify each color. Don't forget to record and date your observations.

My crystal color experience

Crystal _____

Date _____ Time _____

My experience with red _____
_____
_____

My experience with orange _____
_____
_____

My experience with yellow _____
_____
_____

My experience with blue _____
_____
_____

My experience with green _____
_____
_____
_____

My experience with brown _____

_____

_____

My experience with silver _____

_____

_____

My experience with gold _____

_____

_____

My experience with multicolored stones _____

_____

How did the different colors vary in their effect? _____

_____

Which chakras or parts of my body were affected? _____

_____

Did they affect my mood or mental pattern? _____

_____

Was I able to distinguish one color from another with my eyes closed? _____

_____

Experiencing shape

Now that you are beginning to easily experience how crystal energy feels and moves, it is time to move on and experience its effects on and around you and in your environment.

 Exercise 7 WHICH SHAPE AM I?
CD REFERENCE TRACK 2 OR 3 (OPTIONAL)

- **You will need:** a cleansed and activated crystal ball, 7 crystal points, crystal wand or long point, tumbled crystal, geode, cluster, and other crystal shapes

- **Taking each shape in turn**, hold it in your hands and attune to it. Allow yourself to feel how energy circulates in the vicinity of the crystal. Ask yourself if energy is drawn toward the crystal or given out from it.

- **Move the crystal toward and then away** from your body, and try to be aware of the effect that the shape has. Does it pull energy away from you or toward you? Does it feel comforting or disturbing?

- **Now put the crystal somewhere** in your environment, perhaps on your night table. If the crystal has a point, become aware of the difference in energy if the point is facing toward or away from you. Tune into how you feel about the crystal shape being there. Turn it in different directions until it feels comfortable for you. If it feels appropriate, sleep with the crystal in position overnight and see if it makes a difference to how you sleep and what you dream about. Remember to make a record of the results.

- **Now take the seven crystal points** and lie down with them spaced equally around your head, points facing outward. Give yourself five minutes or so to feel how the energy affects you. Then turn the stones point in and again give yourself five minutes or so to experience the energy.

- Holding the crystal wand with the point facing away from you, spiral out from each of your chakras in turn (see page 84). Then turn the crystal point inward (cleansing it first, if appropriate) and spiral back into each chakra (spiral out in whichever direction feels good to you and then back in the opposite direction).

Try the same exercises using the same shapes in a different type of crystal and see how this changes the energy or the feelings you are aware of. Now record your experience in the space provided.

My crystal shape experience

Crystal _____ Shape _____

Date _____ Time _____

When I held the crystal shape it felt _____

The energy was drawn (in or out) _____

When I brought the crystal toward myself I felt _____

When I moved the crystal away from myself I felt _____

When the crystal was in my environment it felt _____

When I turned the crystal around it _____

It affected my sleep and my dreams in this way _____

_____

Did it assist/not assist my dream recall? _____

When I changed the shape of crystal I experienced _____

Crystal _____ Shape _____

Date _____ Time _____

When I held the crystal shape it felt _____

The energy was drawn (in or out) _____

When I brought the crystal toward myself I felt _____

When I moved the crystal away from myself I felt _____

When the crystal was in my environment it felt _____

When I turned the crystal around it _____

It affected my sleep and my dreams in this way _____

Did it assist/not assist my dream recall? _____

When I changed the shape of crystal I experienced _____

_____

Crystal _____ Shape _____

Date _____ Time _____

When I held the crystal shape it felt _____

The energy was drawn (in or out) _____

When I brought the crystal shape toward myself I felt _____

When I moved the crystal shape away from myself I felt _____

When the crystal shape was in my environment it felt _____

When I turned the crystal around it _____

It affected my sleep and my dreams in this way _____

Did it assist/not assist my dream recall? _____

When I changed the type of crystal I experienced _____

Crystal _____ Shape _____

Date _____ Time _____

When I held the crystal points it felt _____

The energy was drawn (in or out) _____

When I placed the points toward my head it felt _____
_____

When I placed the points outward from my head it felt _____
_____

When I changed the type of crystal I experienced _____
_____

Crystal _____ Shape _____

Date _____ Time _____

When I held the crystal shape it felt _____
_____

The energy was drawn (in or out) _____
_____

When I brought the crystal toward myself I felt _____
_____

When I moved the crystal away from myself I felt _____
_____

When I spiraled the wand out from my chakras it _____
_____

When I spiraled the wand in toward my chakras it _____
_____

Exploring crystal systems

Because crystal systems are more subtle than color or form, it can take time to become aware of the effect of their energies, and it is not essential to remember the systems, so this is an exercise to return to as you become more sensitized to crystals. These systems are used in advanced crystal healing, but you can sample their energies by placing the crystals on your solar plexus. Do first check that you have grasped the basic building blocks of the crystal systems by completing the identification exercise below.

Exercise 8 WHAT SYSTEM DO I BELONG TO?
CD REFERENCE TRACK 3 (OPTIONAL)

- **You will need**: a cleansed and activated crystal from each of the eight groups (see pages 63–64 and the Crystal Directory on pages 26–32)

- **Lie down and place a crystal** from the first group on your solar plexus for about five minutes. Notice where in your body, mind, emotions, spirit, or chakras you can feel the effect.

- **Think about whether you are aware** of energy moving from, through, or into the crystal.

- **Record your results** and then repeat the exercise with the next example of a crystal system. Repeat until you have experienced a crystal from each of the eight groups. If you don't resonate with one crystal, try another.

My crystal system experience

Crystal _____ **System** cubic

Date _____ **Time** _____

My thoughts on the effect of this crystal system _____

Energy moved in this direction _____

Crystal _____ **System** hexagonal

Date _____ **Time** _____

My thoughts on the effect of this crystal system _____

Energy moved in this direction _____

Crystal _____ **System** monoclinic

Date _____ **Time** _____

My thoughts on the effect of this crystal system _____

Energy moved in this direction _____

Crystal _____ **System** orthorhombic

Date _____ **Time** _____

My thoughts on the effect of this crystal system _____

Energy moved in this direction _____

Crystal _____ **System** tetragonal

Date _____ **Time** _____

My thoughts on the effect of this crystal system _____

Energy moved in this direction _____

Crystal _____ **System** triclinic

Date _____ **Time** _____

My thoughts on the effect of this crystal system _____

Energy moved in this direction _____

Crystal _____ **System** trigonal

Date _____ **Time** _____

My thoughts on the effect of this crystal system _____

Energy moved in this direction _____

Crystal _____ **System** amorphous

Date _____ **Time** _____

My thoughts on the effect of this crystal system _____

Energy moved in this direction _____

CRYSTALS AND THE CHAKRAS

Chakras and healing

Chakras are centers of energy in the body that distribute our life-force. They connect the physical body with the subtle bodies of the aura around it and with different spiritual dimensions. Traditionally, there are seven major chakras, but more are being re-discovered (see pages 92–96). Each one correlates with a specific crystal and color (although many colors have been assigned to the chakras).

The different chakras govern different aspects of human emotion and behavior, and how well each one is functioning determines whether that aspect of your being is in a state of harmony or disharmony. If a chakra becomes blocked, for example, your flow of subtle energy becomes imbalanced and dis-ease or disharmony on the physical, emotional, mental, or spiritual level eventually results. This makes balancing the chakras an essential base for holistic healing.

To an intuitive eye chakras spin, looking like whirling wheels of light,

although, despite what you might read, there is no one "correct" direction of spin. Dull or black patches or a spin that "wobbles" or is too fast or slow signify dis-ease at the physical, emotional, mental, or spiritual level, according to the chakra concerned. Fortunately, you do not need to "see" such dis-ease because a crystal picks up any disharmony, rectifies it, and re-energizes the chakra.

By placing an appropriate crystal on a chakra, you can ameliorate any negative qualities or specific issues aligned with that chakra or support its positive properties (to find out which positive and negative qualities are associated with the chakras, see the charts on pages 84–87). If you have emotional, mental, or spiritual issues connected to a specific chakra, your overall health will benefit if you place an appropriate crystal on the chakra and leave it there for 20 minutes or so while you relax (you might like to play the music-only track on the CD during your relaxation).

This exercise is suitable for Any crystal that your intuition or a reference book tells you is appropriate for your chakras, but especially Smoky Quartz, Red Jasper, Orange Carnelian, Yellow Jasper, Green Aventurine, Blue Lace Agate, Sodalite, and Amethyst.

Work with your crystals now To cleanse and recharge your chakras, turn to Exercise 9: Full Chakra Cleanse, balance, and recharge on pages 98–99.

I'm not quite there yet Study the chakra charts and diagrams on pages 84–87 until you fully understand the relationship between the chakras and the emotional or mental blocks that can create dis-ease.

THE POSITION OF THE CHAKRAS

1 **Earth chakra** Below feet, grounds into incarnation. Crystal: Smoky Quartz

2 **Base chakra** At the perineum; sexual and creative center. Crystal: Red Jasper

3 **Sacral chakra** Just below the navel; the other sexual and creative center. Crystal: Orange Carnelian

4 **Solar plexus chakra** At the solar plexus; emotional center. Crystal: Yellow Jasper

5 **Heart seed chakra** At the base of the breastbone; site of soul remembrance (see also page 95). Crystal: Danburite

6 **Spleen chakra** Under left armpit; potential site of energy leakage. Crystal: Green Aventurine

7 **Heart chakra** Over the physical heart; love center. Crystal: Rose Quartz

8 **Higher heart chakra** (see page 95) Crystal: Dioptase

9 **Throat chakra** Over the throat; center of truth. Crystal: Blue Lace Agate

10 **Past-life** or **alta-major chakra** Just behind the ears; stores past-life information. Crystal: Variscite

11 **Third eye chakra** Midway between eyebrow and hairline; center of insight. Crystal: Apophyllite

12 **Soma chakra** (see page 95) Crystal: Preseli Bluestone

13 **Crown chakra** At the top of the head; spiritual connection point. Crystal: Amethyst

14 **Soul star** (see page 96) Crystal: Pelalite

15 **Stellar gateway** (see page 96) Crystal: Azeztulite

Note: see also pages 92–96 for the higher vibrational chakras.

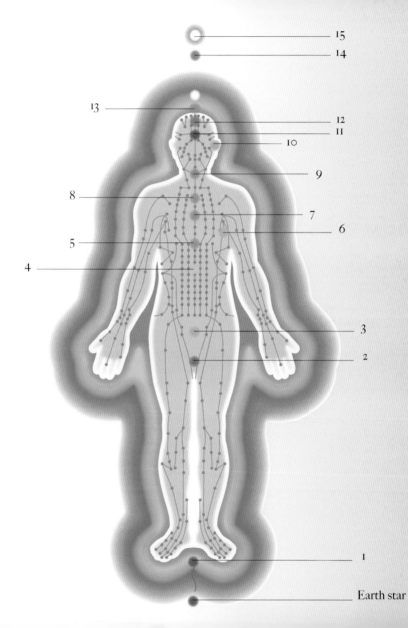

15

14

13

12

11

10

9

8

7

6

5

4

3

2

1

Earth star

CHAKRAS AND THEIR QUALITIES

Earth

COLOR: Brown

POSITION: Below feet

ISSUE: Material connection and grounding

POSITIVE QUALITIES: grounded, practical, operates well in everyday reality

NEGATIVE QUALITIES: no sense of power or potency, cannot operate in everyday reality, picks up negativity

Base

COLOR: Red

POSITION: Base of spine

ISSUE: Survival instincts

POSITIVE QUALITIES: Base security, sense of one's own power, active, independent, spontaneous leadership

NEGATIVE QUALITIES: Impatience, fear of annihilation, death wish, over-sexed or impotent, vengeful, violent, angry, hyperactive, impulsive, manipulative

Sacral

COLOR: Orange

POSITION: Below navel

ISSUE: Creativity and procreation

POSITIVE QUALITIES: Fertility, courage, assertiveness, confidence, joy, sexuality, sensual pleasure, acceptance of sexual identity

NEGATIVE QUALITIES: Low self-esteem, infertility, cruelty, inferiority, sluggishness, pomposity, emotional hooks or thought forms

Solar plexus

COLOR: Yellow

POSITION: Above navel

ISSUE: Emotional connection and assimilation

POSITIVE QUALITIES: Good energy utilization, empathetic, organized, logical, actively intelligent

NEGATIVE QUALITIES: Poor energy utilization, lazy, overly emotional or cold, cynical, has emotional baggage, leaches energy, takes on other people's feelings and problems

Spleen

COLOR: Light green

POSITION: Under left arm

ISSUE: Energy leaching

POSITIVE QUALITIES: Self-contained, powerful

NEGATIVE QUALITIES: Exhausted and manipulated

Heart

COLOR: Green
POSITION: Over heart
ISSUE: Love
POSITIVE QUALITIES: Loving, generous, compassionate, nurturing, flexible, self-confident, accepting
NEGATIVE QUALITIES: Disconnected from feelings, unable to show love, jealous, possessive, insecure, miserly or resistant to change

Throat

COLOR: Blue
POSITION: Throat
ISSUE: Communication
POSITIVE QUALITIES: Able to speak own truth, receptive, idealistic, loyal
NEGATIVE QUALITIES: Incapable of verbalizing thoughts or feelings, stuck, dogmatic, disloyal

Third eye

COLOR: Dark blue
POSITION: Forehead
ISSUE: Intuition and mental connection
POSITIVE QUALITIES: Intuitive, perceptive, visionary, in-the-moment
NEGATIVE QUALITIES: Spaced-out, fearful, attached to past, superstitious, bombarded with other people's thoughts

Past life

COLOR: Light turquoise-green
POSITION: Behind ears
ISSUE: Anything carried over from past lives
POSITIVE QUALITIES: Wise, has life skills, instinctively knowing
NEGATIVE QUALITIES: Carries emotional baggage, insecure, has unfinished business

Crown

COLOR: Violet
POSITION: Top of head
ISSUE: Spiritual connection
POSITIVE QUALITIES: Mystical, creative, humanitarian, giving service
NEGATIVE QUALITIES: Overly-imaginative, illusory, arrogant, exercises power to control others

Chakras and color

Although in modern times chakras have been allocated specific colors based on the colors of the rainbow, the tradition of using crystals on the chakras dates from before these colors were allotted. On very early chakra diagrams, the chakras are shown in various colors, and there were often more than the "traditional" seven chakras.

So when you are working with your crystals, you can either choose to use the modern color correspondences (see right) or to find your own intuitive crystal correspondences. Knowing what alternatives there are is helpful if you want to sedate an overactive chakra. For instance, placing a red crystal on a base chakra that is spinning at full tilt and brimming with lust may only inflame the situation, whereas another color could calm it (although paradoxically Red Jasper often calms this chakra when it is inflamed, so always check the effects for yourself).

Modern chakra color correspondences
Earth Brown
Base chakra Red
Sacral chakra Orange
Solar plexus chakra Yellow
Heart chakra Green
Throat chakra Blue
Third eye chakra Indigo
Crown chakra Purple or white.

 This exercise is suitable for Different-colored crystals associated with the chakras (see above and pages 85–87)

 Work with your crystals now To discover your own color and chakra correspondences, turn to Exercise 10: What Color Are My Chakras? on pages 102–3.

 I'm not quite there yet Return to pages 55–57 to sensitize yourself more fully to crystal colors.

Chakras and the aura

If you have an intuitive eye, you may see an aura as a field of colored lights around the physical body. This vital and energetic energy field is active, vibrating with interweaving layers and multi-colored bands that relate to your physical, emotional, mental, and spiritual states. It is linked to your physical body through the chakras, and if your chakras are balanced and in good order, they strengthen your aura and help to prevent energy "leakage."

The aura delineates "your space." If someone enters your inner auric field, you feel invaded, but energies, thoughts, and feelings can penetrate the aura, even from a distance—and many auras extend into subtle multidimensional fields.

When negative energy, thoughts, or feelings lodge in your aura they cause dis-ease, so cleansing your aura regularly is essential if you are to stay protected and energized. Crystals can also be used to heal "holes" in the aura that arise from causes such as physical scarring or depletion by illness, emotional or mental pain. By strengthening the aura in this way, you make it impossible for other people to penetrate your personal space or leach your energy.

 ➤ **This exercise is suitable for** Flint, Labradorite, Fluorite, Amber, Amethyst, Apache Tear, Black Jade, Bloodstone, Citrine, Tourmaline, Jet, Magnetite, Kunzite, Selenite, Smoky Quartz, and Pyrolusite.

 Work with your crystals now To cleanse, strengthen, and repair your aura, turn to Exercise 11: Strengthening My Aura on page 104–5.

 I'm not quite there yet Revise the method for selecting a crystal intuitively on pages 20–21, asking which crystals would be best for you to use for your aura.

Opening the higher chakras

As we move from the astrological age of Pisces to the age of Aquarius, changes in human consciousness are occurring. New dimensions are opening up, and additional chakras are becoming available to mediate the changing energy and to convert pure consciousness and higher dimensional vibrations into a form that can be assimilated by our earth bodies.

Our physical bodies access these vibrations through the lightbody, one of the subtle bodies held in the aura, and we link with the lightbody through the higher vibration chakras (see the illustration and chart on pages 94–96). Many of the newly discovered crystals work to harmonize the physical body with the lightbody, especially at the neural level.

While it is unwise to force the opening of these higher chakras before you are fully ready, you can prepare your body to receive the new influx of energy and the spiritual insights that accompany it. However, before this new energy can be of any benefit, you need to have worked on clearing any emotional blockages and limiting beliefs, letting go of karmic patterns and overcoming dis-ease. If you try to bypass any of this healing work, suppress issues, or take short-cuts, you will end up ungrounded and open to illusions, delusions, and misinformation because you will not be truly accessing the higher vibrational levels.

Brandenberg

Pink Petalite

Azeztulite

Phenacite

➤ **This exercise is suitable for** Azeztulite, Elestial Smoky Quartz, blue-green Dioptase, pink Danburite, Tugtupeite, golden Danburite, Preseli Bluestone, Petalite, Nirvana Quartz, Phenacite, Brandenberg, or other appropriate high-vibration crystals (see directory on pages 212–17).

Work with your crystals now To open the higher chakras, turn to Exercise 12: Bringing My Higher Chakras On-line on pages 108–9.

Note Undertake this exercise only when you have completed all your healing and therapeutic work.

I'm not quite there yet Continue to work on cleansing your chakras (see pages 98–99), releasing any emotional blocks you may have. If you are unsure about the position of the chakras, see the illustration on page 85, and check out their functions on pages 86–87.

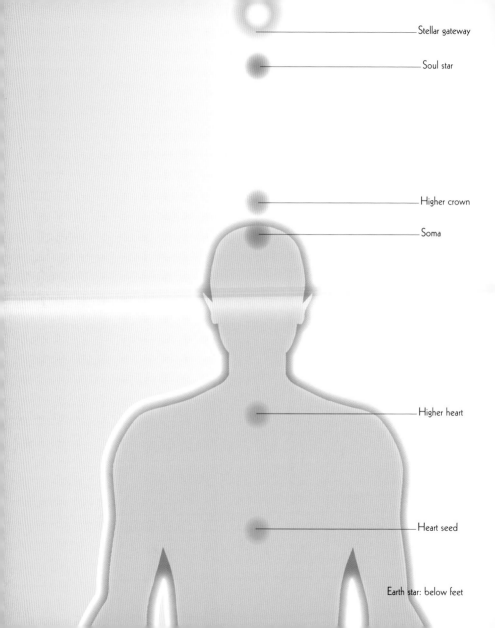

Stellar gateway

Soul star

Higher crown

Soma

Higher heart

Heart seed

Earth star: below feet

HIGHER VIBRATIONAL CHAKRAS

Earth star (higher earth)
COLOR: Brown
POSITION: Below feet
ISSUE: Earth healing
POSITIVE QUALITIES: Grounded, connected to the earth's subtle grid, environmentally aware, and a natural healer
NEGATIVE QUALITIES: Ungrounded, susceptible to environmental pollution, picks up negativity, and creates disharmony

Heart seed
COLOR: Pink
POSITION: Base of breastbone
ISSUE: Soul remembrance
POSITIVE QUALITIES: Remembrance of reason for incarnation, connection to divine plan and tools available to manifest potential
NEGATIVE QUALITIES: Rootless, purposeless, lost, spiritually disconnected, grieving, unable to express feelings, needy

Higher heart
COLOR: Pink or blue-green
POSITION: Over thymus
ISSUE: Unconditional love
POSITIVE QUALITIES: Compassionate, empathic, nurturing, forgiving, spiritually connected
NEGATIVE QUALITIES: Cut off from spiritual nourishment and connectedness

Soma
COLOR: Lavender-blue
POSITION: Center of hairline
ISSUE: Spiritual connection
POSITIVE QUALITIES: Spiritually aware and fully conscious
NEGATIVE QUALITIES: Spaced-out and open to invasion, illusions, and delusions

Higher crown
COLOR: White
POSITION: Several above head
ISSUE: Spiritual enlightenment
POSITIVE QUALITIES: Spiritual, attuned to higher things, enlightened, truly humble
NEGATIVE QUALITIES: Fragmented soul, open to extra-terrestrial invasion

Soul star

COLOR: Lavender/white

POSITION: 1 foot above head

ISSUE: Soul connection and highest self-illumination

POSITIVE QUALITIES: Ultimate soul connection, soul intertwining with physical body together with high-frequency light, communication with soul intention, objective perspective on past lifetimes

NEGATIVE QUALITIES: Invading, messiah-complex, rescues not empowers

Stellar gateway

COLOR: White

POSITION: Above soul star chakra

ISSUE: Cosmic doorway to other worlds

POSITIVE QUALITIES: Connected to highest energies in the cosmos and beyond, in communication with enlightened beings

NEGATIVE QUALITIES: Disintegrated, open to cosmic disinformation, unable to function

CHAKRA EXERCISES

The following exercises will help you to sense and open your chakras and to keep them in good working order. They will also make you aware of your aura and activate the new higher vibration chakras when you are ready to do so.

Sensing and cleansing my chakras

Keeping your chakras balanced and active is essential for good health. You can either do a complete chakra cleanse and recharge, as described here, or you can just cleanse one chakra if you identify with a particular issue or the qualities detailed for that chakra on the chart on pages 84–87. Cleansing a single chakra is also useful if you have an illness or can feel a blockage associated with that chakra. Throat or lung conditions, for instance, respond if you treat the throat chakra, and abdominal distress the base or sacral chakra. For a quick cleanse, take a crystal wand or long point crystal and spiral the energy out from your chakra in one direction (such as clockwise) and then back in again (counter-clockwise). Cleanse the crystal in between if appropriate.

 Exercise 9 FULL CHAKRA CLEANSE, BALANCE, AND RECHARGE

CD REFERENCE TRACK 3 (OPTIONAL)

- **You will need:** cleansed and activated Smoky Quartz, Red Jasper, Orange Carnelian, Yellow Jasper, Green Aventurine, Blue Lace Agate, Sodalite, Amethyst

- **Place the Smoky Quartz** between and slightly below your feet. Lie on your back. Visualize light and energy radiating out from the crystal into your earth chakra for two or three minutes. Be aware that the chakra is being cleansed and its spin regulated.

- **Place the Red Jasper on your base chakra.** Picture light and energy radiating out from the crystal into your base chakra, as before.

- **Place the Orange Carnelian on your sacral chakra**, just below the navel; again picture the light and feel the cleansing process.

- **Place the Yellow Jasper on your solar plexus,** the Green Aventurine on your heart, the Blue Lace Agate on your throat, and the Sodalite on your brow. Each time, visualize the light and feel the cleansing at that chakra.

- **Lastly, place the Amethyst at the crown of your head** and see the light and feel the cleansing at your crown chakra.

- **Now guide your attention slowly from the soles of your feet** up the midline of your body, feeling how balanced and harmonized each chakra has become. Remain still and relaxed, inhaling deep into your belly and counting to seven before you exhale. As you breathe in and hold the breath, feel the energy of the crystals re-energizing the chakras and from there radiating out through your being.

- **When you feel ready, gather up your crystals**, starting from the crown. As you reach the earth chakra, be aware of a grounding cord anchoring you to the earth and into your physical body. Now cleanse your stones thoroughly and record your experiences in the space provided.

Chakra cleanse, balance, and recharge

Date _____ **Time** _____

Crystals _____

Experience _____

_____

_____

_____

_____

_____

_____

Could I sense the energy in my chakras? _____

_____

_____

_____

_____

Were any chakras blocked? _____

_____

_____

_____

_____

Was I aware of any issues or illnesses associated with blocked or non-functioning chakras? (If so work further on this particular chakra later and report the experience here.) _____

_____

_____

_____

_____

_____

_____

_____

_____

_____

If I used a long point crystal, how did it feel? _____

_____

_____

_____

_____

_____

_____

Chakras, crystals, and color

This exercise allows you to find out for yourself to which colors your chakras best respond and which color they naturally exhibit. You can either practice with one of the regular chakras (see pages 82–87) at each session or you could work your way through the whole gamut if you have time.

 ## Exercise 10 WHAT COLOR ARE MY CHAKRAS?
CD REFERENCE TRACK 3 (OPTIONAL)

- **You will need:** a selection of cleansed and activated chakra crystals in different colors.

- **Turn back to pages 70–73 and remind yourself** how you responded to different-colored crystals and whether any of your chakras reacted when you attuned to the various colors.

- **Relax and let your eyes go slightly** out of focus. Taking your attention to each chakra in turn, ask your intuition to tell you which color each one is. You may see the answer as a color or hear the word. (If you find this difficult, finger dowse the color, see page 21.)

- **Working with each of the colored crystals** in turn, hold a crystal close to one of your chakras, move it away, and then bring it near your body again. Notice if this has any physical or subtle effect. Because chakras penetrate far out into the aura, check whether the color changes or deepens the further you move the crystal away from your body.

- **Once you have established a color** for each chakra, repeat the chakra cleanse and recharge from pages 98–101 with the new crystals, noticing what difference the color of the crystal makes, if any.

What colors are my chakras?

Date _____ Time _____

Crystal _____

Chakra	Color	Effect
Earth chakra	_____	_____
Base chakra	_____	_____
Sacral chakra	_____	_____
Solar plexus chakra	_____	_____
Heart chakra	_____	_____
Higher heart chakra	_____	_____
Throat chakra	_____	_____
Brow chakra	_____	_____
Crown chakra	_____	_____

My experience _____

_____

What was different about this experience? _____

_____

Did my chakra colors deepen or change according to how far out in

my aura they were? _____

Did the chakra recharge feel better the first time I did it or

when I changed the colors? _____

Sensing and cleansing my aura

With the assistance of a crystal, you can easily train yourself to sense how far your aura extends and check it for weak spots or for hooks from other people who are pulling on your energy. Ask your intuition to show you which crystals would be appropriate to use. Carry out this exercise regularly.

Exercise 11 STRENGTHENING MY AURA
CD REFERENCE TRACK 3 (OPTIONAL)

- **You will need**: cleansed and activated Smoky Quartz, Red Jasper, Labradorite, Clear Quartz, or Selenite or other aura protection and cleansing crystal (see the Crystal Directory on pages 26–32)

- **Sit on a chair and place the Smoky Quartz** crystal at your feet (point facing outward if it has one). Place the Red Jasper on the chair beneath you, as close to your perineum as possible. Hold the Labradorite in your left hand and the Clear Quartz or Selenite in your right hand.

- **Close your eyes and breathe gently**, focusing your attention on your right hand. Extend your right arm to its full length with your palm facing into your body. Move your hand slowly toward your body. At some point your hand will start to tingle or the crystal will "jump" and you will become aware of your subtle energy field. (This may take a little practice.)

- **Notice how far** the subtle energy field extends from your body. Move your right hand around to see if you can detect any "cold" or weak spots. If you do, hold the crystal over the spot for a few moments.

- **Still holding the crystal** in your right hand, "comb" your body from the top of your head down the front midline of your body to your feet. Repeat, combing down the outside of your body on each side and finally down your back.

- **Notice whether you feel any** "hooks" or "strings" that link your energy to that of someone else—these may be near your body or far out in the aura. If you do, use the crystal to dislodge the hook and send it back where it belongs, then heal the place where it was by holding the crystal over it. Notice too whether you are aware of any thoughts or feelings lodged in your aura and let the crystal gently dissolve these, too.

- **Repeat the "combing"** using the Labradorite in your left hand; this strengthens and seals your aura. Finally, position the Clear Quartz in front of your solar plexus for a few minutes to energize your aura. Remember to cleanse the crystals after use and to record your experiences in the space provided.

My aura cleanse experience

Date _____ **Time** _____

Crystals _____

My experience _____
_____
_____
_____

How did my aura feel? Did I discover any holes or breaks? _____
_____
_____

Were any thoughts or feelings lodged in my aura? _____
_____
_____

Were there any hooks from another person? _____
_____
_____

Did I remove all the thoughts, feelings, and hooks? _____
_____
_____

My aura cleanse experience

Date _____ **Time** _____

Crystals _____

My experience _____

_____

_____

_____

How did my aura feel? Did I discover any holes or breaks? _____

_____

_____

Were any thoughts or feelings lodged in my aura? _____

_____

_____

Were there any hooks from another person? _____

_____

_____

Did I remove all the thoughts, feelings, and hooks? _____

_____

_____

Activating my higher chakras

This exercise helps you to bring your higher chakras "on-line" when you are ready. Make sure that you work slowly and with thought. You may need to repeat the exercise several times before you feel the effect, and it is best not to push yourself. Rather, allow the process to unfold naturally when the time seems right. It can be beneficial to work on one chakra only per session until it is fully activated before moving onto the next one. Remember to close your chakras at the end of the exercise, if appropriate, by picturing shutters closing over them as you remove the crystal. If at any time you feel floaty, light-headed, or dizzy, immediately remove the crystal, close the chakra, and take your attention to the crystal at your feet. Re-anchor yourself by sensing your contact with the earth. Wait for a few days before you try the exercise again.

 Exercise 12 BRINGING MY HIGHER CHAKRAS ON-LINE CD REFERENCE TRACK 3 (OPTIONAL)

- **You will need**: Elestial Smoky Quartz, blue Dioptase, pink Danburite, Tugtupeite, Danburite, Preseli Bluestone, Petalite, Nirvana Quartz, Phenacite, Brandenberg, or other appropriate high-vibration crystals, such as Satyamani and Sayaloka Quartz or Tugtupeite (see the High-vibration Crystal Directory on pages 214–17)

- **Practice Exercise 9, the full chakra** cleanse, balance, and recharge, on pages 98–99 to make sure that your traditional chakras are operating at their maximum efficiency and balance.

- **Place the piece of** Elestial Smoky Quartz or other high-vibration crystal between your feet to activate your higher earth chakra. Then place the blue Dioptase, pink Danburite, or other high-vibration crystal over your higher heart chakra. Wait for a few moments until the crystals and your chakra attune to each other and the chakra opens.

- **Place the Tugtupeite, Danburite,** or other high-vibration crystal on the heart-seed chakra at the base of your breastbone. Wait for a few moments until the crystal and your chakra attune to each other and the chakra opens.

- **Place the Preseli Bluestone** or other high-vibration crystal on the soma chakra at your third eye. Wait for a few moments until the crystal and your chakra attune to each other and the chakra opens.

- **Place the Petalite, Nirvana Quartz,** or other high-vibration crystal a hand's breadth above the crown of your head on the higher crown chakra. Wait for a few moments until the crystal and your chakra attune to each other and the chakra opens.

- **Place the Phenacite, Nirvana Quartz,** or other high-vibration crystal about 1 foot above your head on the soul star chakra. Wait for a few moments until the crystal and your chakra attune to each other and the chakra opens.

- **Place a Brandenberg** or other high-dimension crystal on the stellar gateway above the soul star (see page 96). Wait for a few moments until the crystal and your chakra attune to each other and the chakra opens.

- **Close the chakras, if appropriate, by picturing shutters** closing over each chakra as you remove its crystal. Then picture a big bubble all around you, extending beneath your feet, and visualize the edges crystallizing to protect your newly active chakras. Now record your experiences in the space provided.

My higher chakras crystal activation experience

Date _____ Time _____

Crystal _____ Chakra _____

My experience _____
_____
_____

The most appropriate crystals for me were _____
_____
_____
_____

Date _____ Time _____

Crystal _____ Chakra _____

My experience _____
_____
_____

The most appropriate crystals for me were _____
_____
_____
_____

My higher chakras crystal activation experience

Date _____ Time _____

Crystal _____ Chakra _____

My experience _____

_____

_____

The most appropriate crystals for me were _____

_____

_____

_____

Date _____ Time _____

Crystal _____ Chakra _____

My experience _____

_____

_____

The most appropriate crystals for me were _____

_____

_____

_____

My higher chakras crystal activation experience

Date _____ Time _____

Crystal _____ Chakra _____

My experience _____

_____

_____

The most appropriate crystals for me were _____

_____

_____

_____

Date _____ Time _____

Crystal _____ Chakra _____

My experience _____

_____

_____

The most appropriate crystals for me were _____

_____

_____

_____

CRYSTALS FOR
SELF-DEVELOPMENT

Crystal qualities

In addition to their healing properties, many crystals can offer you support if you would like to nurture specific qualities to benefit your personal development. If you would like to develop more compassion, for example, then wearing, meditating, or sleeping with a Rose Quartz or another heart stone will be of help. If you need to develop more courage, pop a suitably programmed Red Jasper or Red Carnelian into your pocket. If you suffer from anger and need to calm down, avoid red crystals and go for cool pink or green stones, such as Aventurine or Jade. If you constantly criticize yourself, Tiger's Eye can help, and if you are sensitive to criticism Citrine assists, while Kunzite shows how to act on constructive criticism.

You may already be using crystals in this way unconsciously. Many people intuitively or deliberately place crystals over their chakras to release blockages (see pages 82–87) and allow positive qualities to manifest. Look through your crystal collection now—you may find that a number of stones all offer you the same quality, which is evidence that your intuition has drawn you to the right remedy. If this is the case, consciously program the crystal to bring you more of the quality you are seeking (see pages 22–23), then wear the crystal or sleep with it under your pillow for several weeks. From time to time monitor how you are feeling to check whether you need to move on to a different crystal.

Knowing yourself is one of the secrets of a happy and successful life and a Quartz crystal, or any crystal to which you are intuitively drawn, can help you to explore your inner self and the contents of the more hidden parts of your psyche. The crystal shown here, for instance, revealed a troubled childhood and difficult early adulthood, but the phantom and the rainbow at the top pointed the way to happiness and spiritual evolution, drawing on the inner strength developed during those early difficulties.

 **This exercise is suitable for** Any crystal to which you are attracted or that offers you the qualities you are seeking to develop.

Work with your crystals now Turn to Exercise 13: My Quartz Crystal Journey on page 130, remembering to prepare your crystal before you begin (see pages 22–23). The journey can be made in several parts if you wish.

I'm not quite there yet Look up the qualities of the crystals to which you are intuitively attracted in the Crystal Directory on pages 26–32 and see what they tell you about yourself. Alternatively, check out your chakras and the qualities they are associated with on pages 84–87.

Which crystals do I love?

The crystals that you love say a great deal about your personality and your approach to life, and it can be extremely insightful to re-read information on the properties of the crystals in your collection (see the Crystal Directory on pages 26–32) or to think about the type of crystal you tend to go for. If you always pick big, bright and shiny crystals, for example, you are probably optimistic and outgoing—or you might be trying to overcome the needy child element of yourself who wants to feel better by handling pretty, sparkly things.

If all your crystals are a particular color, you may be trying to strengthen the chakra or qualities associated with that color. Light colors can indicate a seeker after spiritual evolution or someone who avoids shadow qualities. If you opt for deep, dark, and intense crystals, you are probably using them to transform your shadow qualities into gifts or protecting yourself against negative thoughts and feelings that may come from outside yourself.

Looking deeply into the qualities of the crystals to which you are attracted is an excellent way to learn more about the unconscious urges you harbor within yourself and to develop the positive side of your personality.

This exercise is suitable for Any crystal to which you are attracted or which you wear regularly.

Work with your crystals now To learn what the crystals to which you are attracted say about you, turn to Exercise 14: What Do the Crystals I Love Tell Me? on page 134.

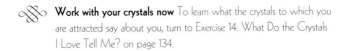

I'm not quite there yet Study the properties of the crystals in your collection further.

Lemurian Jade

Blue Moonstone

Greenlandite

Mystic Topaz

Merlinite

The crystals you choose to wear say a
great deal about your personality.

Which crystals do I avoid?

There are two main reasons for avoiding particular crystals (apart from cost): either you don't like the look of the crystal or you have responded badly when wearing or handling one previously. This could be a clue to something you are trying to hide from yourself. It might be a feeling or an attitude you deem to be "bad" and have suppressed deep within your subconscious, or perhaps the crystal is having a cathartic or detoxifying effect that is a little too strong for you. In either case, allowing yourself to explore the cause of your aversion and gently drawing off the feelings with a crystal such as Smoky Quartz will make you feel much better. Once you have drawn off the initial source of distress, you may require the support of a crystal that instills the opposite quality.

The Smoky Elestial crystal pictured opposite was deeply disliked by one of my workshop participants—she said it looked like "an angry snake waiting to pounce." Having worked with the crystal, she realized that it was bringing back the memory of a flasher jumping out of the bushes when she was a small child. Smoky Elestial Quartz is a beautiful crystal for transmuting the depression and fear such a traumatic memory can cause, and it reminded her that her gift of swift feet had carried her to safety.

 This exercise is suitable for Any crystal to which you have an aversion or any traumatic memory you wish to release.

 Work with your crystals now To learn how you can bring hidden memories and traumatic or undesirable feelings to the surface for release, turn to Exercise 15: Facing My Shadow Energy on pages 138–39.

 I'm not quite there yet Sit quietly holding one of the "soft" crystals, such as Rose Quartz or Rhodochrosite, that dispel fear until you feel able to work with the avoided crystal.

How can I protect myself with crystals?

Psychic self-protection is essential if you are to work sensibly with crystals—and for other reasons too. Other people's energies and thoughts can quickly deplete your energy. Electromagnetic smog and geopathic stress also affect how well you can work with your crystals because, if you don't take steps to prevent it, you can pick them up as

negative energies that lodge in your aura or your organs. Family members or partners can also create stress in each other. So, what do you do about it?

Well, crystals are brilliant at providing protection and creating safe spaces, drawing off negative energies and keeping energy pirates at bay. By keeping your energy as high as possible, you will also be able to attune to high-vibration crystals when you are ready, raising your own vibrations to reach multidimensional spaces.

Remember when seeking protection from crystals to cleanse them regularly, especially if you are wearing them or they are out in your environment (see pages 22–23). Also, be aware that you can wear or place crystals to block negative energies from reaching you. For example, placing crystals such as Rose Quartz or Labradorite near a party wall if you have noisy or intrusive neighbors calms them down almost immediately. Wearing a Black Tourmaline when you've annoyed someone or are the object of their jealousy protects you, absorbing ill-wishing and bringing peace to your life once more.

The spleen protector

If you feel exhausted in someone's company, or wilt when she or he phones you—especially if you have an ache under your left armpit—then this person is drawing on your energy field via your spleen chakra.

You will find that a spleen protector soon sorts out such energy pirates, and, as a general rule, green crystals, such as Jade, Fluorite, and Gaspeite, work well for the spleen chakra. There are other crystals that can be used to provide similar protection for your solar plexus (protecting you from emotional draining), your liver (from other people's anger invading you), your kidneys (from other people's fear invading you), and so on.

 This exercise is suitable for Any form of energy depletion you experience; choose your crystal by intuition or from the references in the Crystal Directory on pages 26–32.

 Work with your crystals now To cut off energy drains, turn to Exercise 16: Protecting My Spleen on page 140.

 I'm not quite there yet Play track 1 of the CD, relax, and take your mind back to situations in which you always feel tired or experience sudden energy depletion. This will help you to identify energy pirates and adverse situations.

DIRECTORY OF PROTECTION CRYSTALS

Fluorite, Amazonite, or Quartz Neutralize electromagnetic smog; place clusters by the computer or TV.

Green Fluorite

Smoky Quartz Absorbs geopathic stress and negative energies of all kinds and protects against energy drains.

Smoky Quartz

Turquoise Clears environmental pollution and assists personal protection.

Turquoise

Labradorite Separates your energy from other people's thoughts and feelings so that you are able to retain an empathetic yet objective perceptive viewpoint.

Labradorite

Black Tourmaline

Black Tourmaline Deflects ill-wishing and protects against electromagnetic smog; tape one to your mobile phone.

Sodalite

Green Aventurine and Sodalite Protect against electromagnetic smog.

Bloodstone

Amber or Bloodstone Cleanse negative energies and protect the aura.

Selenite

Selenite Draws spiritual energies to create a safe, sacred space.

Rose Quartz

Rose Quartz or Amethyst Replace negativity with positive, loving vibrations; place against the wall to calm intrusive energies or emotional angst.

Protecting my space

Crystal grids are the perfect way to safeguard your space because they create an energetic net. They also create a safe holding space while you journey or conduct rituals. In fact, by positioning your crystals in ordered grids rather than placing them randomly, you can enhance all your space, by keeping the areas cleansed and energized.

There are many shapes of grid, so experiment with them in order to work out which one makes you feel good. Experiment too with the crystals you use. Dowsing is an excellent way to both choose and position your crystals (see pages 20–21).

Remember that crystals used in this way require regular cleansing. After cleansing them, re-connect them using a wand. (If the gridlines pass through a wall, take the wand up to the wall and then around to the other side, where the line continues.)

 This exercise is suitable for All protective crystals, but especially those on page 123.

 Work with your crystals now To check out which grids are beneficial for you, turn to Exercise 17: Using Grid Systems on page 142. Select the stones and their exact positioning by finger or pendulum dowsing.

 I'm not quite there yet Check out the protective properties of crystals in the Crystal Directory on pages 26–32 and then revise your finger-dowsing technique (see page 21).

Dowsing pendulum

CRYSTAL GRIDS

Triangulation

You will need:

- 3 cleansed and activated crystals
- Crystal wand

Triangulation gridding works well to neutralize negative energy and bring in positive energy. Place one crystal centrally along a wall and two others on the wall opposite at an equal angle if possible. If you are working on a whole house, the lines of force pass through walls, so connect the points with a wand to strengthen the grid.

Zig-zag

You will need:

- 8 cleansed and activated crystals
- Crystal wand

The zig-zag layout is particularly useful for dealing with sick building syndrome and environmental pollution. Place appropriate crystals as shown on the diagram, remembering to return from the last stone laid to the first. Cleanse the stones regularly.

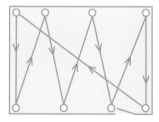

Five-pointed star

You will need:

- 5 cleansed and activated stones
- Crystal wand

This is a useful protection layout or caller-in of love and healing, and it enhances your energy. Follow the direction of the arrows on the diagram when placing crystals and remember to return to the start crystal to complete the circuit. Like the Star of David (see page 128), this layout can be used to grid around a body and also for a room or other space.

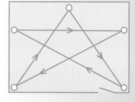

Figure-of-eight

You will need:

- 6 cleansed and activated high-vibration stones
- 6 cleansed and activated grounding stones

This layout draws spiritual energy down into the body and melds it with earth energy drawn up from the feet to create perfect balance. It also opens a cosmic anchor to ground you between the core of the earth and the galactic center, creating core-energy solidity that equips you to ride out energetic changes and channel high-vibration energy down to earth. Place high-vibration stones, such as Amphibole, Cacoxenite, and Blue Moonstone, above

the waist to the crown of the head, and grounding stones, such as Poppy Jasper, Agate, and Septarian, below the waist, down to the feet. Remember to complete the circuit back to the first stone that you placed.

Star of David

You will need:

- 6 cleansed and activated crystals
- Crystal wand

The Star of David is a traditional protection layout but it also creates an ideal manifestation space when it is laid with large Grossular Garnet, Ammolite, or other abundance stones. Lay the first triangle and join up the points, then lay another triangle the other way up, over the top. Join up the points. If you are using Bronzite and Black Tourmaline to neutralize ill-wishing, lay the Bronzite triangle first and cleanse the star daily.

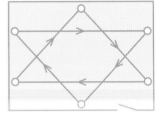

SELF-DEVELOPMENT EXERCISES

The exercises in this section will help you to raise your vibrations and enhance your sensitivity to crystals while encouraging you to take on new qualities that support your self-development. They also assist you in keeping your personal and environmental energies high, clean, and safe.

What can crystals tell me about myself?

This journey takes you deep inside yourself to experience your ego and your unique sense of self. You will find out what makes you *you* and how you can express your individuality. The journey then moves you out to see how you fit into the wider picture. This helps you to harness your ability to innovate, to lead, and to follow your own path with courage. This journey can be undertaken in shorter sections if you find it too much to do at one time. Simply pause the CD when you need to, but always follow the close-down at the end each time you complete a section and remember to date your experience.

Exercise 13 MY QUARTZ CRYSTAL JOURNEY
CD REFERENCE TRACK 4 (TO FOLLOW THE SCRIPT, TURN TO PAGES 246–247)

- **You will need**: a cleansed and activated crystal intuitively selected from your crystal collection; a Quartz crystal is ideal, but be guided by your intuition

- **Play Track 4 of the CD now** and follow the instructions for your Quartz crystal journey. After completing your journey, record your experience in the space provided.

My Quartz crystal journey experience

Date _____   Time _____

Crystal _____

My experience _____

_____

_____

_____

What drives my ego and my desires? _____

_____

_____

_____

How do I assert myself? _____

_____

_____

_____

How do I express this in my day-to-day life? _____

_____

_____

_____

What areas of life do I procrastinate in? _____

_____

_____

_____

_____

Where am I totally self-absorbed? _____

_____

_____

_____

_____

What is the difference between my ego and my Self? _____

_____

_____

_____

_____

What was it like to be part of the whole and then to become a unique

individual again? _____

_____

_____

_____

How did it feel to birth my Self? _____

_____

_____

_____

_____

What is my pathway? _____

_____

_____

_____

_____

What were the gifts in my shadow? _____

_____

_____

_____

_____

What were the gifts I left for myself? _____

_____

_____

_____

_____

What do my crystals tell me?

If it contains a preponderance of certain colors or types of crystal, then your crystal collection may say a great deal about the type of qualities you value or are trying to attract to yourself. This exercise will help you to explore this.

Exercise 14 WHAT DO THE CRYSTALS I LOVE TELL ME?

- **You will need:** 4 or 5 cleansed and activated crystals of various shapes and/ or colors

- **Take a close look** at your crystal collection. If it contains several crystals of one particular color, turn to page 88 and check out which chakra this color resonates with, then look at pages 86–87 to find out which qualities and characteristics are associated with that chakra.

- **Now turn to the Crystal Directory** on pages 26–32 or *The Crystal Bible* and read about the qualities of all your favorite crystals. Does a common theme run through the descriptions? If so, what does this say about you?

- **Look at the crystals illustrated** on page 117. Which pendant would you like to wear? Read on to find out what this says about you: Mystic Topaz is optimistic and outgoing and likes to dazzle; Merlinite is restrained, discerning, and self-contained; Blue Moonstone is mystical and intuitive; Greenlandite is dependable and calm; Lemurian Jade is protective and mysterious. Now record your experience in the space provided.

My crystal collection experience

Date _____ Time _____

Crystals _____

_____

_____

_____

My experience _____

_____

_____

_____

_____

_____

_____

_____

_____

_____

_____

_____

_____

_____

Did a particular color or theme run through my crystals? _____

_____

_____

_____

_____

_____

Did my crystals tie into a particular chakra? _____

_____

_____

_____

_____

If so, having read the qualities associated with that chakra, how does this apply to me

either positively or negatively? _____

_____

_____

_____

_____

_____

What positive qualities do my crystals bring to me? _____

_____

_____

_____

_____

_____

Which crystal particularly attracted me on the illustration? _____

_____

_____

_____

_____

_____

What were its properties? _____

_____

_____

_____

_____

_____

_____

oming aversion

with any crystals placed at your feet, such as
sion or Smoky Quartz or Hematite, help to
you draw off and detoxify traumatic feelings
he of or memories. You can also hold Rose
e Quartz to calm your fear.

Exercise 15 FACING MY SHADOW ENERGY

- **You will need:** A crystal to which you have an aversion, Smoky Quartz or Hematite (if you have an aversion to these crystals, substitute clear Quartz), plus a heart-healing crystal or one that instills the positive side of the aversion (see the Crystal Directory on pages 26–32)

- **Place the Smoky Quartz or Hematite** (or clear Quartz) between your feet.

- **Now hold the crystal to which you** have an aversion; if the aversion is really strong, place the stone on a table in front of you. Ask yourself what it is you dislike so much about this stone. Is it the color? The shape? The feelings you get when you look at it? Ask yourself where you feel the aversion: in your hands, your heart, or your gut? Does it make you feel sick or your back squirm?

- **Breathe gently and calmly, taking the breath** right down into your belly. Ask the crystal to talk to you—to communicate with you to help you identify where this aversion stems from inside yourself. What memories does it bring up or which attitudes does it represent? Ask the crystal to help you gently release and heal these negative feelings.

- **When you have finished exploring** the negative feelings, take the heart-healing or postive crystal and hold it over your heart. Breathe gently into the crystal so that

the energy flows into your heart. Tap the crystal gently over your heart
and repeat to yourself several times, "I forgive myself for having this
feeling/memory/aversion, and I unconditionally love and accept myself for
having had it. I release myself now." Now write up your experience in the
space provided.

My crystal aversion experience

Date _____ Time _____ Crystal _____

My experience _____

_____

_____

What the crystal symbolized _____

_____

Crystals used to heal it _____

_____

How I feel now _____

_____

_____

Protecting myself

Crystallizing the outer edges of your aura, provides some protection from energy pirates and other sappers of your subtle energy, but to further ensure that no one can pull on your energy, use this exercise to protect your spleen. Experiment with the different crystals mentioned until you find exactly the right one for you and, if you suffer from extreme energy depletion, keep the stone taped over your spleen.

Exercise 16 PROTECTING MY SPLEEN

- **You will need:** Green Fluorite, Green Aventurine, Jade, or other spleen crystal, plus Quantum Quattro or another power stone (see pages 214–17)

- **Tape one of the crystals** over your spleen chakra (about a hand's breadth beneath your left armpit). This immediately cuts off hooks from energy pirates.

- **Now picture a large**, three-dimensional pyramid extending down from the spleen chakra just below your left armpit to your waist on the back and front of your body. Give the pyramid a floor. This will protect your spleen further.

- **To re-empower yourself,** replace the crystal with the Quantum Quattro or one of the other power stones.

- **To protect yourself in other way**s, repeat the crystal-and-pyramid set-up using red crystals over your liver (for protection from other people's anger), yellow crystals over your solar plexus (for protection from those desperate for emotional nourishment), or green or pink crystals over your heart (protection against picking up someone's heartbreak). Now record your experience in the space provided.

My spleen protection experience

Date _____ **Time** _____

Crystals _____

My experience _____

_____

_____

_____

The best crystal to protect my spleen was _____

_____

_____

The best crystal to protect my liver was _____

_____

_____

The best crystal to protect my solar plexus was _____

_____

_____

The best crystal to protect my heart was _____

_____

_____

Protecting my environment

Carefully positioning crystals into a grid provides you with a safe, peaceful, and energetically clean space in which to live, love, work, play, and meditate. Remember to join the crystals with a wand to complete the grid.

Exercise 17 USING GRID SYSTEMS

- **You will need:** a selection of protective gridding crystals (see pages 126–28), plus a wand

- **Study the grids on pages 126–128** to find out which shape you intuitively respond to. Begin by laying out that grid on the floor, as shown. Join up the crystals with the wand and then stand in the center to see how the grid feels.

- **Try out all the grids in turn,** varying the crystals as appropriate.

- **When you find the grid and crystals** that resonate best with your energies, lay that grid around your home, room, or workspace and leave it in place. Now record your experience in the space provided.

My crystal gridding experience

Date _____ Time _____

Crystals _____

Grid shape _____

Effect on me _____

_____

Date _____ Time _____

Crystals _____

Grid shape _____

Effect on me _____

_____

Date _____ Time _____

Crystals _____

Grid shape _____

Effect on me _____

_____

Date _____ Time _____

Crystals _____

_____

Grid shape _____

Effect on me _____

_____

Date _____ Time _____

Crystals _____

_____

Grid shape _____

Effect on me _____

_____

Date _____ Time _____

Crystals _____

_____

Grid shape _____

Effect on me _____

_____

HOW CAN I BE MY OWN CRYSTAL HEALER?

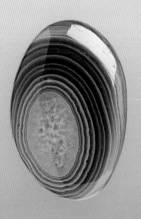

Sources of dis-ease

Dis-ease is a state of disequilibrium that results from physical imbalances, blocked feelings, suppressed emotions, toxic thoughts, or environmental stress (caused by excess electromagnetic stimulation or "sick building syndrome"). If left unchecked, dis-ease can finally result in physical illness. Because healing means bringing back into balance, crystals are an excellent way to treat dis-ease, since they gently correct imbalances in the body, emotions, mind, aura, and the chakras (see pages 82–87).

Everyone has the potential to be a crystal healer, and it is easy to stimulate your own self-healing by placing crystals on or around your body. This can include wearing a crystal for long periods of time, or placing or taping a crystal over an organ for a shorter period.

The immune system

Your first lines of defense against the invasion of dis-ease and organisms such as viruses or bacteria are your physical and psychic immune systems. Lack of balance in the physical immune system can lead to illness. If this system is underactive, for example, viral infections such as colds and flu may result. If it is overactive, you could be prone to rheumatoid arthritis or lupus. A dysfunctional physical immune system is a common response to environmental, emotional, mental, or physical stress. A disturbance in the psychic immune system is usually caused by toxic emotions or thoughts or by ill-wishing, negative environmental energies and blocked chakras.

To discover whether your immune systems are out of balance, you can dowse (see pages 20–21) or judge for yourself the reaction of your immune system to a specific crystal. Then you can restore balance by stimulating or calming both your immune systems via the thymus gland, situated in the center of your chest, about a hand's breadth below your collarbone. To enhance your physical immune system, place a piece of Smithsonite at each corner of your bed and tape a Green Tourmaline or Bloodstone over your thymus, leaving it in place overnight. To enhance your psychic immune system, try placing Black Tourmaline, Brandenberg Amethyst, or Selenite over your thymus.

Immune stimulators

Environmental stress Bloodstone, Smithsonite, Amethyst, Clear Quartz, Green Aventurine

Emotional stress Rose Quartz, Danburite

Mental stress Sodalite, Green Tourmaline

Viruses Fluorite, Cathedral Quartz, Amphilbole

Auto-immune system Paraiba or other Tourmaline

Make a note of any other crystals that you find effective in the exercises that accompany this chapter.

 This exercise is suitable for Any of the crystals mentioned above or which you intuitively choose.

 Work with your crystals now To explore the effect of crystals on your immune system turn to Exercise 18: Finding My Immune-system Crystal on pages 162–63.

 I'm not quite there yet Turn to pages 82–87 to revise the information on crystals and the chakras, or turn to pages 152–57 to find out about crystals and the organs.

Crystals and my emotions

Using crystals is an excellent way to balance your moods and transmute negative emotions into positive ones. So often the dis-ease is caused by toxic emotions and repressed feelings that we unwittingly hold onto when they are long past their "sell-by date." Since these emotions are so deep, we have no idea what is causing our inner distress. Crystals winkle out these hidden vulnerabilities, gently bringing them to our attention and showing us how to find the gift held within them—the signpost to emotional well-being.

Toxic emotions can be held within the heart, the chakras, or aura, and so placing appropriate crystals on these points is extremely beneficial. You may need to repeat the placement daily or to tape the crystals in place for several days while the underlying cause of the dis-ease surfaces. Then you may require another crystal to help you heal—you can intuitively finger dowse this crystal (see page 21) or read up on the properties of the crystals detailed in the Crystal Directory on pages 26–32 or in either volume of *The Crystal Bible*. You can also use Gem Essences (see pages 190–92) to heal emotional dis-ease.

This is by no means a definitive list of healing crystals for the emotions, but it will help you to start turning your emotional dis-ease into emotional well-being. Make a note of other crystals you find effective in the exercises that accompany this chapter.

HEALING CRYSTALS FOR EMOTIONS

Powerlessness
CHAKRA: Earth
CRYSTAL: Smoky Quartz
POSITIVE EMOTION: Empowerment

Insecurity
CHAKRA: Base
CRYSTAL: Red Jasper
POSITIVE EMOTION: Security

Low self-esteem
CHAKRA: Sacral
CRYSTAL: Orange Carnelian
POSITIVE EMOTION: Self-confidence

Inferiority
CHAKRA: Solar plexus
CRYSTAL: Yellow Jasper
POSITIVE EMOTION: Empathy

Resentment
CHAKRA: Base and Heart
CRYSTAL: Rhodorite
POSITIVE EMOTION: Appreciation

Jealousy
CHAKRA: Heart
CRYSTAL: Green Aventurine
POSITIVE EMOTION: Compassion

Neediness
CHAKRA: Higher heart
CRYSTAL: Rose Quartz
POSITIVE EMOTION: Unconditional love

Disloyalty
CHAKRA: Throat
CRYSTAL: Blue Lace Agate
POSITIVE EMOTION: Loyalty

Self-delusion
CHAKRA: Brow
CRYSTAL: Sodalite
POSITIVE EMOTION: Emotional clarity

Arrogance
CHAKRA: Crown
CRYSTAL: Clear Quartz
POSITIVE EMOTION: Joy

Releasing from the past

Do you have any Rainbow Obsidian or any other banded crystal among the crystals in your collection? If so, you have selected the perfect tool to release yourself from the past. You intuitively chose this crystal because you are holding onto something that is detrimental to your current well-being and because this crystal will offer insight into the gifts that lie at the heart of the situation.

If your lover has left you and you are having difficulty letting go, for instance, wearing beautiful Rainbow Obsidian or Rhodochrosite over your heart will sever the cords of old love, encouraging you to move on. These crystals help you to recognize the lessons you have learned, the inner strengths you have drawn on, and the qualities you have developed during the relationship. If you have things to say that you never dared say before, feelings to express or creative energy to manifest, then gentle Blue Lace Agate can assist you.

Any banded crystal is perfect for facilitating such a journey of self-discovery. While undertaking the journey deep into your self you may see clear pictures, experience physical or emotional feelings, or simply *know*, and insights become clearer as you write them down, so keep a record in the journal section of this book.

Blue Lace Agate

Malachite

Banded Agate

Rainbow Obsidian

➤ **This journey is suitable for** Banded or Whorled Jaspers, Banded Agate, Botswana Agate, Blue Lace Agate, Tiger's Eye, Hawk Eye, Malachite, Rhodochrosite, Phantom Quartzes, Ammolite, Chrysotile, Shaman Quartz, Charoite, Nebula Stone, Rhyolite, Sugilite; assessing the properties of any whorled or banded crystal.

Work with your crystals now Turn to Exercise 19: My Rainbow Obsidian Journey on page 166, remembering to prepare your crystal before you begin (see pages 22–23). The journey can be made in several parts if you wish.

I'm not quite there yet If you don't feel tuned into a healing crystal, go to Exercise 4: Attuning to My Crystals on pages 44–45.

Crystals and my organs

Many crystals resonate with specific body organs and can be used to support healing and to bring an organ back into balance. You can either place the crystal over the chakra closest to the organ or over the organ itself, then leave it in place for 15–20 minutes. Crystal layouts can also be extremely useful for detoxifying your organs (see page 170).

Much early crystal healing came about because of notions of similarity and correspondence: stones that looked like an organ or a condition were used to cure it. Bloodstone, which is green and red, has been used for 5,000 years to heal the blood and blood-rich organs and to strengthen the kidneys. It is still used today, like Snakeskin Agate, a very wrinkled crystal used to overcome skin conditions.

Physical and subtle anatomy

Knowing where your organs lie within your body allows you to position crystals for maximum effect. If you already know about the body's energy meridian systems you can also utilize these for crystal healing.

This exercise is suitable for Bloodstone, Amethyst, Red Jasper, Smoky Quartz, Sodalite, Yellow Jasper, and other detoxing stones.

 **Work with your crystals now** To experience a crystal detox, turn to Exercise 20: My Detox Layout on page 170.

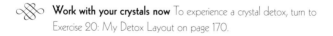 **I'm not quite there yet** Study the physical anatomy diagram opposite to learn where your organs are, or turn to pages 82–87 to check out your chakras and make sure there are no blockages.

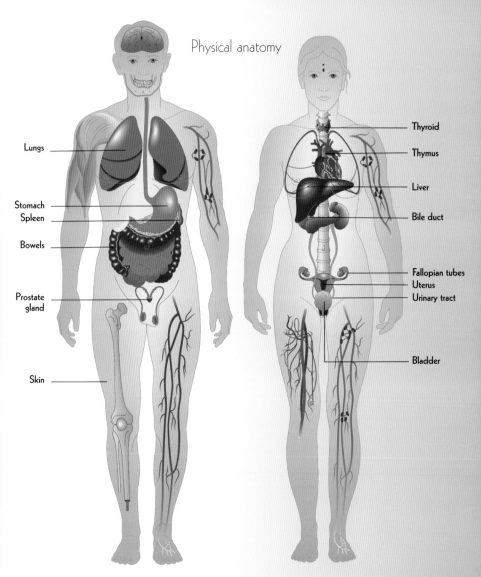

Physical anatomy

Lungs

Stomach
Spleen

Bowels

Prostate
gland

Skin

Thyroid

Thymus

Liver

Bile duct

Fallopian tubes
Uterus
Urinary tract

Bladder

Subtle anatomy

The various layers of the
aura interweave and may
appear as different colors
to an intuitive eye.

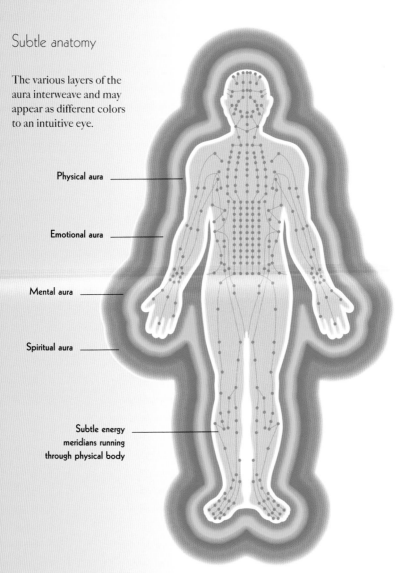

Physical aura _____

Emotional aura _____

Mental aura _____

Spiritual aura _____

Subtle energy _____
meridians running
through physical body

THE DETOXIFICATION LAYOUT

If your body is overloaded with toxins it cannot maintain good health. Stimulating your liver by using the detoxification layout releases toxins and encourages your lymphatic system to remove them, bringing about a physical cleansing. Placing a Yellow Jasper on your solar plexus brings about an emotional detox as well, while if you feel that your mind needs detoxing, add crystals such as Fluorite or Sodalite.

You can adapt the detoxification layout given on page 170 to work on different organs by changing the crystals. Choose those that correspond with the organ you wish to rebalance by looking at the list on pages 156–57 and position them appropriately.

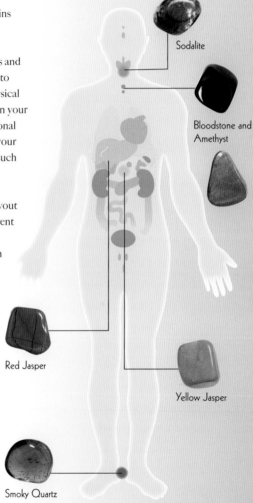

Sodalite

Bloodstone and Amethyst

Red Jasper

Yellow Jasper

Smoky Quartz

DIRECTORY OF ORGAN AND CRYSTAL CORRESPONDENCES

This list is in no way definitive, and you can add more crystals to it from the crystals that you find effective in the exercises that accompany this chapter.

Bile duct Jasper, Gaspeite, Jade

Bladder and urinary tract Amber, Jasper, Jade, Orange Calcite, Yellow Zincite, Bloodstone

Bowels Jasper, Amber, Ruby, Clear Quartz, Iron Pyrite, Bloodstone

Brain Lapis Lazuli, Fluorite, Magnesite

Endocrine system Amazonite, Amber, Amethyst, Tourmaline, Jasper, Citrine, Fire Agate, Green Quartz, Tanzine Aura Quartz

Eyes Blue Lace Agate, Sapphire, Chrosoprase, Aquamarine, Vivianite

Fallopian tubes and uterus Chrysoprase, Moonstone, Flint

Jasper

Amber

Iron Pyrite

Snakeskin Agate

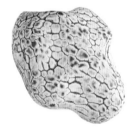

Lapis Lazuli

Gall bladder Carnelian, Gaspeite, Jasper, Topaz, Jade

Liver Amethyst, Tugtupeite, Aquamarine, Beryl, Bloodstone, Charoite, Jasper, Jade, Topaz, Gaspeite

Lungs Rhodochrosite, Chrysocolla, Turquoise, Iron Pyrite

Lymphatic system Tourmaline, Zincite, Halite

Pancreas Pink Opal, Serpentine

Prostate gland Chrysoprase

Skin Snakeskin Agate, Sapphire, Aquamarine

Spleen Green Aventurine, Green Fluorite, Apple Aura Quartz, Green Jade

Stomach Agate, Fire Agate, Turquoise, Lapis Lazuli

Thymus Smithsonite, Bloodstone

Thyroid Tanzine Aura Quartz, Rhodochrosite, Sodalite

Crystals and my mind

Because it secretes mood-altering substances, the brain has a powerful effect on the way we feel. However, you can take control of your mind, and learning to invoke the creativity and clarity of crystal energies helps to reprogram your brain and mind to work to its best advantage.

Crystals can affect how clearly you think and how well you analyze situations. They also calm an overactive mind and invigorate a sluggish one. Keeping a Bloodstone in your pocket during examinations, for instance, helps you to focus and overcomes brain fatigue. Wearing a crystal as earrings or as close as possible to your head or popping one under your pillow at night is another excellent way to keep your mind focused. Crystals that release toxic thoughts or beliefs that no longer serve you or that help you to overcome deeply ingrained patterns of thinking would make effective earrings. You can also use crystal layouts to bring about specific results (see the illustration here and the exercise on page 174).

 This exercise is suitable for Any of the crystals mentioned on page 160 or which you choose intuitively.

 Work with your crystals now To boost your memory and powers of concentration, turn to Exercise 21: Improving My Mind on page 174.

 I'm not quite there yet Read through all your journal entries so far in the exercises within each chapter. Can you spot any ingrained thoughts or beliefs running through your experiences? Do any of the crystals mentioned on page 160 suggest solutions?

Improving my mind layout

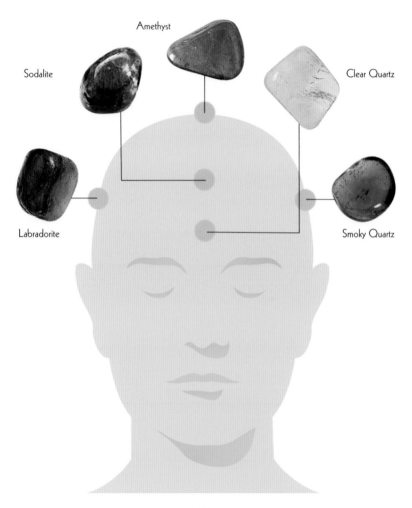

Amethyst

Sodalite

Clear Quartz

Labradorite

Smoky Quartz

CRYSTALS FOR THE MIND

This is not intended to be a definite list, and you can add crystals as you discover more about their mind-enhancing properties. Make a note of the crystals you find effective in the exercises that accompany this chapter.

Concentration, focus, memory, and learning Amethyst, Carnelian, Labradorite, Clear Quartz, Fluorite, Smoky Quartz, Sodalite, Bloodstone

Decision making and lateral thinking Amethyst, Bloodstone, Chrysocolla, Rose Quartz

Creativity Green Aventurine, Jasper, Rose Quartz, Sodalite

Calming mental stress Blue Lace Agate, Celestite

Dissolving rigid mental conditioning Sodalite

Dealing with addictions Amethyst

Overcoming depression Kunzite, Sunstone

Resolving midlife crises Rose Quartz

Tackling panic attacks Sodalite, Rose Quartz

Dealing with neurosis Green Aventurine

Combatting over-sensitivity Sodalite, Amethyst, Black Tourmaline

Turning negative thoughts to positive ones Smoky Quartz, Sunstone

HEALING EXERCISES

The exercises in this section will help you to keep your mind, immune system, body, and emotions in peak condition so that you enjoy well-being and ease.

Crystals for healing myself

Select two or three crystals from the list of immune-system stimulators on page 147 and cleanse them thoroughly (see pages 22–23). You can finger dowse for these or choose them intuitively (see pages 20–21). As an example you might choose Bloodstone because it's a good all-round healing crystal that stimulates or sedates the immune system as required, Fluorite because it's a good viral healer that guards against colds and flu, or Sodalite because you're harboring obsessive, toxic thoughts that are stressing you out as they emerge just before you go to sleep or as you wake up during the night.

 Exercise 18 FINDING MY IMMUNE SYSTEM CRYSTAL CD REFERENCE TRACK 3 (OPTIONAL)

- **You will need:** 2 or 3 cleansed and activated immune-stimulating or other healing crystals (see above)

- **Relax and tune into your thymus** at the center of your chest, about a hand's breadth down from your collarbone in the same way as you would tune into a crystal (see pages 44–45). Does your thymus feel over-stretched, rapid, and racing or does it feel sluggish and slow to react?

- **Consider what might be causing** you stress. If you wish, choose an additional crystal and put it in the appropriate place.

- **Taking each crystal in turn,** place it over your thymus gland. Leave it in place for 10–15 minutes and notice how your body responds. Do you feel more relaxed, does your mind slow down or does a wave of well-being sweep through your body? How does your thymus respond: does it slow down or speed up?

- **Do you become aware** of any other parts of your body needing support—the spleen, for instance, which is an important part of the immune system? If so, find an appropriate crystal, such as Green Aventurine, which protects against psychic vampires who pull on your energy to feed their own.

- **Try tapping the crystal seven times**, either over your thymus or alongside it on both sides. Notice whether this strengthens the effect of the crystal.

- **Once you have established** your favorite immune-stimulating crystal, place it over your thymus and lay a Clear Quartz on the center of your forehead whenever you would like to stimulate your immune responses. Place your hands in the crease of your groin on both sides. Relax for 10 minutes. (Repeat daily for 1 week.) Alternatively, gently tap the immune-stimulating crystal over your thymus. Now record your experience in the space provided.

My immune-stimulating experience

Date _____   Time _____

Crystals _____

My experience _____

_____

_____

_____

_____

How did my thymus feel? _____

_____

_____

_____

_____

Am I suffering from stress? If so what kind? _____

_____

_____

_____

_____

_____

Which immune-stimulating or immune-sedating crystals work best for me? _____

_____

_____

_____

Does tapping with a crystal work well for me? _____

_____

_____

_____

What effect did stimulating my immune system for a week have? _____

_____

_____

_____

Did the quality of my sleep improve? _____

_____

_____

What are my other major causes of stress and which crystals would help me

overcome them? _____

_____

_____

Releasing myself from the past

This exercise has been designed for use with Rainbow Obsidian, but any banded crystal that you have tuned into will be equally effective. No matter how busy your life is, be sure to allow enough time and space for this journey.

You can either play this journey through from beginning to end and then write up your experience or pause the CD at the musical interludes while you record your experience at each stage.

 ## Exercise 19 MY RAINBOW OBSIDIAN JOURNEY
CD REFERENCE TRACK 5 (TO FOLLOW THE SCRIPT, TURN TO PAGES 248–49)

- **You will need:** a cleansed and activated Rainbow Obsidian or other banded crystal

- **Play Track 5 of the CD now** and follow the instructions for the Rainbow Obsidian journey. Then record your experience in the space provided.

My Rainbow Obsidian journey experience

Date _____   Time _____

Crystal _____

My experience _____
_____
_____
_____
_____

Why did I choose this crystal? _____
_____
_____
_____
_____

How was my past affecting my present? _____
_____
_____
_____
_____
_____

What did I need to let go? _____

_____

_____

_____

_____

_____

_____

How easy was it to forgive? _____

_____

_____

_____

_____

_____

Would another crystal have helped this process? _____

_____

_____

_____

_____

_____

What gifts did I discover? _____

_____

_____

_____

_____

_____

_____

How can I put them to work in my life? _____

_____

_____

_____

_____

_____

What other properties did the crystal have? _____

_____

_____

_____

_____

_____

My crystal layouts

If you are able to enlist the help of a friend for this exercise, ask him or her to lay the crystals onto you in the order stated. If you have to do the exercise alone, lay the lower stones first at your feet and solar plexus, then lie down and put the others in place. You can adapt this layout to work on other organs and the crystals they correspond with (see pages 156–57). To recap on the site of your organs, see the illustrations on page 153.

 ## Exercise 20 MY DETOX LAYOUT
CD REFERENCE TRACK 3 (OPTIONAL)

- **You will need**: Bloodstone, Amethyst, Red Jasper, Smoky Quartz, Sodalite, Yellow Jasper, or other detoxing stones of your choice

- **Lie down comfortably and relax**. Lay the Bloodstone and Amethyst over your thymus.

- **Lay the Red Jasper over your liver** (at the base of your ribs on your right side).

- **Lay the Smoky Quartz** between your feet.

- **Lay the Sodalite** at the base of your throat.

- **Lay the Yellow Jasper** over your solar plexus. Relax here for 10–20 minutes.

- **Remove the stones and thoroughly cleanse them**. Drink plenty of water over the next 24 hours. Now record your experience in the space provided.

My detox layout experience

Date _____   **Time** _____

Crystals _____

_____

My experience _____

_____

_____

_____

How I felt before the layout _____

_____

_____

How I felt immediately after the layout _____

_____

_____

How I felt 24 hours later _____

_____

_____

_____

Other crystal layout experiences

Date _____ **Time** _____

Crystals _____

_____

Reason for layout _____

_____

Immediate effect _____

Effect after 24 hours _____

_____

Date _____ **Time** _____

Crystals _____

_____

Reason for layout _____

_____

Immediate effect _____

Effect after 24 hours _____

_____

Date _____ Time _____

Crystals _____

_____

Reason for layout _____

_____

Immediate effect _____

_____

Effect after 24 hours _____

_____

Date _____ Time _____

Crystals _____

_____

Reason for layout _____

_____

Immediate effect _____

_____

Effect after 24 hours _____

_____

Crystals for my mind

Crystals can be an enormous support for the mind, and a simple layout can help you to think more clearly and improve your memory. This exercise makes a big mental difference. Before beginning, look back at the map for this simple layout on pages 158–59. You might like to familiarize yourself with the position of the chakras too, shown on pages 84 and 95–96. Repeat the layout every day for a week and vary the stones if you intuitively feel this is appropriate.

 ## Exercise 21 IMPROVING MY MIND
CD REFERENCE TRACK 3 (OPTIONAL)

- **You will need:** cleansed and activated Amethyst, Sodalite, Clear Quartz, Labradorite, and Smoky Quartz tumbled stones

- **Lie down comfortably and place** the Amethyst above your head (at the crown chakra).

- **Place the Sodalite high on your forehead** (over the soma chakra), then place the Clear Quartz lower on your forehead (over the third eye).

- **Place the Labradorite to your right** and the Smoky Quartz to your left.

- **If you have a problem that needs a solution,** think about it for a moment or two and ask for a solution, then forget all about it. Close your eyes and relax with the crystals in place for 10–20 minutes. If you had a problem, let the solution rise into your mind at the appropriate time.

- **Gather up your crystals and stand up slowly,** grounding yourself as you do so by becoming aware of a cord anchoring you to the earth and into your physical body. Now record your experience in the space provided.

My mental improvement experience

Date _____ Time _____

Crystals _____
_____
_____
_____

My experience _____
_____
_____
_____
_____
_____
_____

How did I feel during the laying of the crystals? _____
_____
_____
_____
_____
_____

Did a solution to my problem become immediately apparent? _____

_____

_____

_____

_____

_____

How has my memory been since doing the layout? _____

_____

_____

_____

_____

Has repeating the layout for a week improved my concentration? _____

_____

_____

_____

_____

_____

HOW DO I KEEP MY CRYSTALS WORKING?

Working with crystals every day

The most important way to keep your crystals working for you is to cleanse, energize, and reactivate them regularly. Remember that if you don't ask your crystals to work with you, they will be unsure of their role in your life. The more you work with your crystals, the more your energies will mesh and your stones will pick up an unspoken request in a heartbeat. The best way to ensure this is to talk to and handle your crystals every day. Working with them as often as possible and keeping them around you helps you to live in the crystal world. Respecting your crystals also helps.

Crystals are alive—they have sentience and knowing—and if you honor this and respect their knowledge, they will work even harder for you in return. One of the nicest ways to work daily with your crystals is to put them in your bath (see page 180) or to meditate with them (see page 194). When you are meditating you can create a crystal mandala or focus on one special crystal —once you have done the meditation a few times, your brainwaves will automatically drop into the pattern most conducive for meditation as soon as you pick up your meditation crystal.

 This exercise is suitable for Any crystal, but crystal balls or crystals that have planes, flaws, and inner landscapes are excellent meditation tools because they provide a focus for your attention and keep your mind busy while your consciousness changes.

 Work with your crystal now To meditate with your crystal, turn to Exercise 22: Traveling My Inner Planes on page 194.

 I'm not quite there yet Play Track 1 on the CD and follow the instructions for relaxation, focusing, and opening.

Crystal bathing

Taking a bath with your crystals is a wonderful experience. Some crystals, such as Halite, dissolve in the water, giving you a thorough energetic cleanse and revitalization. Other crystals give you a crystal love experience.

To create a crystal love bath, prepare the room carefully. Light a rose-scented candle in a Rose Quartz candle holder because rose is the perfume of Venus, the goddess of love. Add a few drops of rose oil to the bathwater if you wish. Spritzing suitable gem essences around the room adds to the ambience, too (see pages 190–92). Use Venus crystals in your bathwater. Rose Quartz is the Goddess of Love's favorite, but Danburite, Larimar, Rhodonite, and many other crystals carry her energy.

Either place them in the water or add them as a gem essence. Delicate crystals are best placed around the rim of the bath to avoid damage or disintegration.

When you are in the bath, lie back, close your eyes and let the water gently lap around you, carrying the crystal vibration deep into your skin. Massage around your heart and belly with a crystal. Allow yourself at least 20 minutes and preferably longer to immerse yourself in the crystal vibration, opening your heart to love. As you dry yourself, thank the crystals for their assistance and then carefully dry them.

Rose Quartz

Crystal massage

Crystal wands with gently rounded ends, eggs, or tumbled stones make excellent massage wands to gently release tension and infuse you with the qualities of the stone. Use Rose Quartz to give yourself unconditional love and forgiveness, Rhodonite to gently erase memories of abuse, Rutilated Quartz to lift you from a dark mood, Carnelian, Clear Quartz, or Red Jasper for all-over revitalization, Amethyst to bring you to a spiritual high, Angelite for an angelic experience, or any other crystal that feels good to you.

Massage the crystal gently over your whole body or as much of it as you can reach. If you have a partner who is willing to massage you with the crystal, so much the better. Sharing the effects of one of your favorite crystals with your lover or friend in this way is a deeply intimate experience, especially if you give massage as well as receive it.

This exercise is suitable for Any rounded or tumbled stone; it is not appropriate to use a pointed crystal for massage.

Work with your crystal now For a soothing crystal massage, turn to Exercise 23: Giving Myself a Crystal Massage on pages 196–97.

I'm not quite there yet Go out and buy yourself a massage wand or crystal egg that really speaks to you.

Amethyst—use round end

Rose Quartz—use round end

Talking to your crystals

The more you talk to your crystals the more they respond to you—and even though you may laugh at the idea of talking to a crystal, remember that whenever you ask a crystal to work with you, you are talking to it. When you attune to a crystal, you are allowing it to speak to you. This "talking" can take place out loud or in your mind. Telepathy with a crystal works really well once you have attuned to that specific crystal and has the advantage of pulling in the assistance of the crystal whenever you need it, no matter how far the distance between you. This is particularly powerful if you are in the habit of meditating with your crystals because you can ask the crystal to assist you during your meditation and then forget all about it until you need the crystal input.

You can, of course, carry your crystals with you, either by wearing them or keeping them in your pocket. As you handle them talk to the crystals in your mind. Don't be surprised if they start to talk back to you!

 This exercise is suitable for Talking to any of your crystal collection, but this exercise is particularly useful for bi-colored crystals, such as Merlinite, Zebra Stone, Gaspeite, Atlantasite, Dalmation Stone, Jasper, Rhodonite, or crystals that balance yin and yang.

 Work with your crystals now To learn to talk to your crystal and find inner balance, turn to Exercise 24: Finding My Inner Balance on pages 198–99. You can apply the principles to any talk you wish to have with your crystals.

 I'm not quite there yet Turn back to page 44 and attune yourself to your crystals.

Bi-colored stones

Graspeite

Atlantasite

Dalmation Stone

Shiva Lingham

Jasper

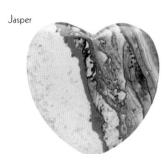

Merlinite

Incorporating new spiritual qualities

The clearer and lighter your own vibrations become, the more closely you can attune yourself with crystals, the more your spiritual gifts will open, and the greater will be the increase in your sensitivity.

Crystals have a deep desire to share the wisdom they have gathered over millions of years in the earth, and they can provide you with spiritual guidance.

Much of this guidance comes through dreams and signals, and the more sensitive you are, the more you can become aware of these subtle signs. You can also use the exercise on page 202 to draw specific qualities to yourself, such as compassion, unconditional acceptance and forgiveness, or universal love. All you need to do is select the right crystal to bring that quality or spiritual gift to you (see pages 188–89).

This exercise is suitable for Chrysoprase or Dioptase for compassion; Mangano Calcite, Chrysoberyl, Chrysoprase, Apache Tear, Rhodonite, Infinite Stone, Okenite, Rose Quartz, Rutilated Quartz, Sugilite, Rhodochrosite, or Tugtupite for forgiveness; or any other crystal that opens you to spiritual gifts or qualities (see pages 188–89).

Work with your crystals now To open your intuition and spiritual insight, turn to Exercise 25: Accessing My Spiritual Gifts on page 202.

I'm not quite there yet Spend time reading and thinking about the information on pages 188–89.

Spiritual gifts layout

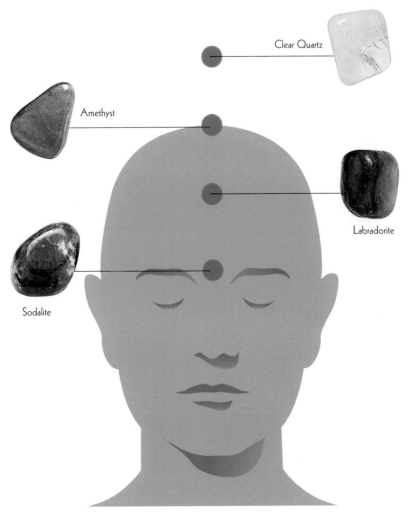

Clear Quartz

Amethyst

Labradorite

Sodalite

DIRECTORY OF CRYSTALS FOR SPIRITUAL GIFTS

Intuition Knowing things without having to fathom out the reasoning or logic; intuition puts disparate information together and makes a great leap. A subtle sensing takes place in your body or heart, then communicates the information to your mind.
INTUITION-ENHANCING CRYSTALS:
Apophyllite, Selenite, Labradorite, Amethyst, Yellow Calcite, Angels Wing Calcite, Lapis Lazuli, Azurite, Moonstone, Star Sapphire, Amazonite, Celestite, Sodalite, Smoky Quartz, Lavender Smithsonite, Azeztulite, Petalite, Phantom Quartz, Ametrine, Aqua Aura, Kyanite, Apatite, Antacamite

Inner wisdom Often referred to as the voice of the heart or soul. Attuning to your inner wisdom involves stilling the everyday mind and shutting off stimuli from the outer world. In the silence, you access your own knowing.
WISDOM-RETRIEVING CRYSTALS: Cathedral Quartz, Record Keepers, Lemurian Seed, Phantoms, Elestials, Serpentine, Snow Quartz, Herkimer Diamond, most high-vibration stones

Telepathy Intentionally—and sometimes unintentionally—passing thoughts, words, pictures, and symbols from one mind to another without verbalization or visual clues; can operate over vast distances.
TELEPATHY-ENHANCING CRYSTALS:
Angelite, Chalcedony, Herkimer Diamond, Selenite, Phantoms, Elestial, and other Quartzes

Precognition Moving forward in time to access knowledge about the future.
VISION-ENHANCING CRYSTALS: Peridot, Moldavite, Petalite, Azeztulite, Libyan Desert Tecktite, Azurite

Retrocognition Moving backward in time to access knowledge about the past, including past-life memories.
VISION-ENHANCING CRYSTALS: Peridot, Moldavite, Petalite, Azeztulite, Libyan Desert Tecktite, Azurite, Variscite, Eudialyte

Psychokinesis Moving objects by the power of the mind alone.
PSYCHOKINESIS-ENHANCING CRYSTALS:
Quartz, Amber

Remote viewing Also known as astral traveling or journeying. The ability of consciousness to leave the physical body and travel to another place, bringing back a report of what it sees there.
JOURNEYING-ENHANCING CRYSTALS: Shaman Quartz, Phantoms, Avalonite, Brandenberg, Prasiolite, high-vibration stones

Clairvoyance Information received through impressions, thoughts, pictures, and symbols. Communication is often with another level of existence, such as the spirits of those who have departed, but can involve reading the contents of a sealed envelope and such like.
CLAIRVOYANCE-ENHANCING CRYSTALS: Yellow Labradorite (Bytownite), Quartz, Apophyllite, Azurite with Malachite, high-vibration crystals

Clairaudience Information received through a distinct voice—often heard behind the ear—or by an idea "popping" into the mind.
CLAIRAUDIENCE-ENHANCING CRYSTALS: Dumortierite, Geothite, Orange River Quartz, Phantom Quartz

Clairsentience The subtle gift of receiving information from a flower or similar object through sensing.
CLAIRSENTIENCE-ENHANCING CRYSTAL: Preseli Bluestone

Psychometry Ability to read the impressions retained by objects or places.
PSYCHOMETRY-ENHANCING CRYSTAL: Preseli Bluestone

Channeling (trance) A spirit or being who is no longer on earth (or who, it is claimed, is extraterrestrial) who communicates through the medium of a living person using his or her voice box or by passing information into the mind.
CHANNELING-ENHANCING CRYSTALS: Moldavite, Celestite, Apophyllite, Bustamite, Calcite Fairy Stone, Cavansite, Quantum Quatro, Drusy Quartz, high-vibration crystals

Automatic writing When words appear without thought; the feeling that something outside oneself is writing.
WRITING-STIMULATING CRYSTALS: Chinese Writing Stone, Calligraphy Stone

Gem essences

Because crystals work by resonance and vibration, their energy can pass into water—as a gem essence—and then into your body. You can make gem essences from a single crystal or a combination, then add an essence to bathwater, rub it on your skin, disperse it around your aura with your hands, spray it around a room, or take a few drops three times a day.

Remember to always use cleansed and activated stones when making essences. Use the indirect method for toxic or friable stones. These include Malachite, Galena, Stibnite, Tiffany Stone, Bornite, Beryllium, Halite, Selenite, and all fragile crystals. If you are unsure whether a crystal is toxic or friable, use a tumbled crystal and the indirect method.

Making a gem mother essence: direct method

First ascertain whether the crystal is toxic (see above; if you suspect it might be toxic, use the indirect method described on page 192). Then cleanse your crystal (see pages 22–23).

Place the cleansed crystal in a clean glass bowl and cover with pure spring water. Place the bowl in the sunlight for up to 12 hours (cover if necessary). Some essences enjoy being out in the moonlight or during a rain storm. Remove the crystal from the water.

If the essence is to be stored for more than two days, pour the water into a clean glass bottle until one-third full. Make a mixture of two-thirds brandy or vodka and one-third spring water and use to top up the bottle. Clearly label the bottle with the name of the essence and date. This is a mother essence or tincture. Store in a cool, dark place and dilute before use by adding 7 drops to a bottle of one-third brandy to two-thirds water. This is a stock bottle. Dilute again with 7 drops to one-third brandy and two-thirds spring water (see page 204).

Note Do not take toxic crystal essences by mouth.

Making a gem mother essence: indirect method

Cleanse your crystal (see pages 22–23). Place the cleansed crystal in a small, clean glass bowl and stand this bowl in a larger bowl.

Pour pure spring water into the outer bowl only. Place the bowls in sunlight for up to 12 hours (cover if necessary).

Remove the water from the outer bowl and follow the instructions for the direct method on page 190.

 ➤ **This exercise is suitable for** Any crystal but check whether it is toxic or fragile before making the essence and, if so, use the indirect method (see above). To make a protection essence, use Black Tourmaline, Smoky Quartz, Green Aventurine, or other protective stones that remove negativity.

 Work with your crystals now To make a healing gem essence, turn to Exercise 26: Using My Gem Essence on page 204.

 I'm not quite there yet Turn back to pages 146–60 to check out the healing properties of the crystals you are considering using to make a gem essence.

EXERCISES TO KEEP CRYSTALS WORKING

These exercises will help you to deepen your connection with your crystals, raise your spiritual awareness, and open your intuition further. They will also help you to incorporate new qualities into your spiritual development and to try out gem essences.

Meditating with crystals

Before starting crystal meditation, make sure that you will not be disturbed, turn off your phone, and dim the lights. You can sit in any position you find comfortable. Remember to cleanse your crystal before use (see pages 22–23).

 ## Exercise 22 TRAVELING MY INNER PLANES
CD REFERENCE TRACK 3 (OPTIONAL)

- **You will need:** a cleansed and activated crystal ball or a crystal with inner planes, flaws, phantoms, or a landscape

- **Sit comfortably and hold your crystal or ball** loosely in your hands or place it on a table in front of you with your hands resting on it. Relax and let your eyes go slightly out of focus. Breathe gently into your belly so that you establish a natural, slow rhythm.

- **Let your eyes softly follow** the inner planes of your crystal or ball, journeying all around the crystal until you feel calm, peaceful, and centered.

- **When you are ready, close your eyes** and allow that peace to take you deep into yourself to a place of absolute stillness and silence.

- **Again, when you are ready,** bring your attention back out to the ball or crystal. Open your eyes, look at the crystal and thank it for its assistance. Take your hands away from the ball, disconnecting from the crystal energy.

- **Feel your feet placed firmly** on the floor and your sitting bones on the chair. Visualize a crystal bubble extending all around you, protecting your aura. Stand up and stretch. Now record your experience in the space provided.

My inner plane experience

Date _____ **Time** _____

Crystal _____

My experience _____

_____

_____

_____

_____

_____

_____

_____

_____

_____

_____

_____

_____

_____

_____

_____

_____

_____

_____

_____

_____

Experiencing a crystal massage

Crystal massage is a very gentle experience and one that allows you to really feel the energy of the crystal and the love it has for you. Choose your crystal in accordance with what you wish to receive from the massage (see the Crystal Directory on pages 26–32) and remember to cleanse and activate the crystal before you start (see pages 22–23). The most potent time to practice this exercise is at the full moon or the dark of the moon.

 Exercise 23 GIVING MYSELF A CRYSTAL MASSAGE
CD REFERENCE TRACK 3 (OPTIONAL)

- **You will need**: a cleansed and activated crystal massage wand or tumbled stone

- **Lie in a warm place** where you will not be disturbed. You can either massage over your clothes or onto your skin, whichever feels more comfortable.

- **When you are comfortably settled**, repeat the feeling-safe affirmation to yourself three times: "I am safe, I am loved, I trust myself and my crystal."

- **Take your crystal** and hold it in your hands, asking that it helps you to relax and heal (or whatever else you want from the massage). Feel the loving energy of the crystal warming your hands and passing through your body.

- **When you feel ready**, gently stroke the crystal all over your body; you may like to begin with your hands or feet. Use circular massage movements or sweeping strokes, whichever feel more comfortable and pleasurable.

- **Use the crystal to explore your body fully**. Take your time. Notice which areas feel least comfortable, lay the crystal gently there and allow the healing energies of the crystal to make this part of your body feel good.

- **Keep stroking and massaging** your body with the crystal until your whole body is glowing with the pleasure of crystal love.

- **When you are ready** to end the massage, lie quietly for five minutes and then get up slowly. Have a good stretch and move around or simply go to sleep with your massage crystal beneath your pillow. Don't forget to record your thoughts in the space provided.

My crystal massage experience

Date _____   Time _____

Crystal _____

My experience _____

_____

_____

_____

_____

_____

_____

Listening to your crystals

The following exercise helps your crystal to speak back to you! Do not use music for this exercise: you need to be fully aware of your crystal speaking. All of us have a balance of masculine and feminine energy within us, and this exercise helps you to find equilibrium.

Choose a bi-colored crystal that has as equal a balance of the two colors as possible. The Shiva Lingham on page 185 is somewhat more feminine than masculine, for instance, but is highly suitable for feminine working since its masculine shape brings balance.

Exercise 24 FINDING MY INNER BALANCE

- **You will need:** a cleansed and activated bi-colored crystal, such as a Shiva Lingham (see page 185).

- **Holding your Shiva Lingham** in both hands, ask it to help you find inner balance.

- **Taking your Shiva Lingham** in your left hand, place the lighter colored part on the left side of your body, wherever feels intuitively right (you can move it around if you wish). You may wish to start with your head and then work down your body.

- **Ask the Shiva Lingham** to tell you how your feminine energy works, how receptive, nurturing, and giving you are, and how you use your powers of assertion. If you are working down your body, you can ask at the mental level (your head), at the emotional level (your heart and solar plexus), and at the active level (your belly).

- **Listen for the answer** in your heart or slightly behind your physical ear, where your inner ear lies.

- **Now place the darker end** of the Shiva Lingham wherever feels comfortable on the right side of your body. Ask the crystal to tell you how you use your masculine energy, how assertive and active you are, and how much you initiate and protect. Listen for the answer as before.

- **Finally, take the Shiva Lingham** in both hands and place it on the midline of your body—you may want to move through each major chakra in turn, starting at your belly (see pages 84—85).

- **Ask the crystal to help you** find a point of balance between your masculine and feminine energy. When you reach that point of balance, rest quietly in its stillness.

- **Then ask your crystal to speak.** Don't forget to record your experience in the space provided.

My finding balance experience

Date _____ Time _____

Crystal _____

My experience _____

_____

_____

_____

_____

_____

How easy was it to hear my crystal speak? _____

_____

_____

_____

_____

Was my feminine or masculine energy stronger? _____

_____

_____

_____

_____

Do I think in a masculine or feminine way? _____

_____

_____

_____

_____

Do I assert myself in a masculine or feminine way? _____

_____

_____

_____

_____

How did it feel to reach a point of balance? _____

_____

_____

_____

What did my crystal say in the silence? _____

_____

_____

_____

_____

Incorporating new spiritual qualities

This exercise helps you to open your intuition and access other spiritual gifts. It is a useful meditation that slowly opens your third eye and enhances your ability to see beyond the everyday. Once you have done the layout shown on page 187, vary the crystals to see which opens your third eye most easily. You can vary the exercise by replacing the Labradorite with Bytownite or Spectrolite (higher resonances of the basic crystal) or with an Apophyllite pyramid or other intuition-enhancing crystal (see page 188). You can also use crystals to help you journey out of your body, to open clairvoyance, or to assimilate spiritual qualities into your life (see page 188–89).

 ## Exercise 25 ACCESSING MY SPIRITUAL GIFTS
CD REFERENCE TRACK 3 (OPTIONAL)

- **You will need**: cleansed and activated Clear Quartz, Amethyst, Labradorite, Sodalite, or other intuition-enhancing crystals

- **Lie down comfortably** and place the Clear Quartz above your head.

- **Place the Amethyst** so that it is just touching the crown of your head. Place the Labradorite at the top of your forehead and Sodalite between your eyebrows.

- **Close your eyes** and take your attention to your third eye. Leave the crystals in place for 15 minutes and note the effect on your third eye and your intuition.

- **When you have finished** gather up the crystals, stand up, and ground yourself firmly by becoming aware of a grounding cord anchoring you to the earth and into your physical body. Picture shutters closing over your third eye to protect it.

My intuition-opening experience

Date _____   Time _____

Crystals _____

_____

My experience _____

_____

_____

_____

Other crystals I tried _____

_____

Effect _____

_____

_____

_____

_____

How is my intuition working now? _____

_____

_____

_____

Healing with gem essences

Before starting this exercise, ask yourself for what healing purpose you would like to make a gem essence. Do you want to bring balance to your physical body, your mind, or your emotions, or do you have a more spiritual goal? Perhaps you would like to use the essence as a room protection spray. When you have decided on your purpose, select the appropriate crystal or crystals from pages 146–60, cleanse and activate them (see pages 22–23), and then make the mother essence following the direct or indirect method on pages 190–92.

Exercise 26 USING MY GEM ESSENCE

- **You will need**: mother essence (made from cleansed crystal(s), clean glass bowl, spring water), small dropper bottles, brandy or vodka, spring water

- **Make a dosage bottle**: take 7 drops of the mother essence and place into a small dropper bottle. Top up with one-third brandy or vodka to two-thirds spring water. This is a stock bottle, and it will keep for several weeks in a cool, dark place. Clearly label and date it.

- **Make a dosage or spray bottle**: take a further 7 drops from the stock bottle and add them to a new bottle. Top up with one-third brandy or vodka to two-thirds spring water. (If making a spray for immediate use, omit the brandy.)

- **To use the essence**, finger dowse (see page 21) to ask whether you should take the essence under your tongue (7 drops), over a chakra or affected organ, or disperse it into your aura, your environment, or your bathwater. Use the essence three times a day as directed for at least a week and preferably longer, recording your experience in the spaces provided.

My gem essence experience

Date essence made _____ **Date** _____

Crystal(s) _____

Purpose _____

_____

_____

Effect _____

_____

_____

Date essence made _____ **Date** _____

Crystal(s) _____

Purpose _____

_____

_____

Effect _____

_____

_____

Date essence made _____ Date _____

Crystal(s) _____

Purpose _____

_____

_____

Effect _____

_____

_____

_____

Date essence made _____ Date _____

Crystal(s) _____

Purpose _____

_____

_____

Effect _____

_____

_____

_____

Date essence made _____ Date _____

Crystal(s) _____

Purpose _____

_____

_____

Effect _____

_____

_____

_____

Date essence made _____ Date _____

Crystal(s) _____

Purpose _____

_____

_____

Effect _____

_____

_____

_____

Date essence made _____   Date _____

Crystal(s) _____

Purpose _____

_____

_____

Effect _____

_____

_____

_____

Date essence made _____   Date _____

Crystal(s) _____

Purpose _____

_____

_____

Effect _____

_____

_____

_____

TAKING CRYSTAL
WORK FURTHER

Working with higher vibration crystals

High-vibration crystals have a finer, lighter, and more refined vibration than the crystals used so far in this book. Their energy connects both to higher dimensional realities and to your core spiritual identity, bringing about multi-dimensional healing and spiritual alchemy. These crystals stimulate new chakras now coming on-line, such as the soul star and stellar gateway (see pages 92–96), while working with the traditional chakras to accommodate their high-frequency energies. Most high-vibration stones work slowly to bring about physical change because they act on the subtle levels of being first and are more suitable for multidimensional work.

Having one of these "high vibes" stones in your collection could be extremely beneficial if you are consciously working to embody spiritual energies, raise your vibrations and activate your lightbody, or open the higher chakras. Some of these stones are unique, "one-off" crystals, such as Tugtupite or Tanzanite (a member of the Zoisite family), some are a colored variation of a basic crystal like Rainbow Moonstone, or Paraiba Tourmaline, but others may be a specific form of Quartz, such as Azeztulite, or Quartz that has been alchemically enhanced, such as the Aura Quartzes.

Note You should only begin to work with a high-vibration crystal when your vibrations are in harmony with the crystal. It is important to have completed your healing and evolutionary work in this earth dimension first and to have worked through all the previous exercises in this book.

This exercise is suitable for Rainbow and Blue Moonstone, Selenite, Azeztulite, Petalite, Danburite, Golden and Aqua Aura Danburite, Paraiba Tourmaline, Tanzanite, Natrolite, Mystic Topaz, Ajoite, Beryllonite, Stellar Beam Calcite, Purple Scapolite, Tugtupite, Greenlandite, Brandenberg Amethyst, Spectrolite, Herderite, Tanzine and other Aura Quartzes, Vera Cruz Amethyst and Super 7, Elestial, Lemurian, Sichuan, Celestial, Spirit, Indicolite, Nirvana, Satyalokan and Sayamani Quartz, or other high-vibration crystals.

Work with your crystal now To compare high- and low-vibration crystals turn to Exercise 27: Comparing My High- and Low-vibration Crystals on page 226. Then to attune yourself to these crystals turn to Exercise 28: Attuning to My High-vibration Crystals on page 228.

I'm not quite there yet Turn to pages 92–96 to find out more about opening your higher chakras or to enhance your ability to feel crystal energies turn to page 44.

Tanzine Aura Quartz

Paraiba Tourmaline

Tugtupeite

HIGH-VIBRATION CRYSTAL DIRECTORY

This directory is not a definitive guide, and there are other high-vibration crystals that you might like to work with (see *The Crystal Bible* volume 2). Write your experiences in the spaces on pages 229–31 as you discover them.

Brandenberg (trigonal; clear, amethyst, smoky) In my opinion, the crystal that has everything, Brandenberg connects to the perfect blueprint that has been there since before time began. Excellent for all inter-dimensional work and for accessing high vibrations, opening all the new chakras.

Brandenberg

Danburite (orthorhombic; pink, lilac, or golden) The perfect heart-healer, Danburite can transport you to higher dimensions to connect to your higher self and angelic guidance, especially in its golden form. It assists with karmic healing, equipping you to break away from the past and follow your soul path. Facilitates emotional detoxification on all levels.

Pink Danburite

Celestite

Celestite (orthorhombic; blue) Strongly connected to the angelic realm, Celestite is a higher dimension teacher that will kick start your spiritual enlightenment. Sharpens the mind and assists communication.

Spectrolite

Labradorite/Bytownite/Spectrolite/Hypersthene (triclinic; blue-green-gray, yellow, lilac) Perfect for separating your energy from that of another person and deflecting psychic attack. Labradorite is an excellent protector for the aura.

Bytownite, Spectrolite, and Hypersthene are more refined vibrations of this mystical crystal. They open psychic gifts and higher chakras and ground spiritual insights.

Tanzanite

Tanzanite (orthorhombic; purple) An excellent journeying tool, Tanzanite facilitates altered states of consciousness and is an ascension crystal. Assists in multidimensional cellular and karmic healing and helps you to find your vocation.

Azeztulite (trigonal; white, colorless, golden-yellow) A light-bearer, Azeztulite works at the spiritual level, creating chakra connections to higher reality and expanding consciousness. It facilitates a vibrational shift by bringing higher frequencies down to earth and raising your personal vibration. You then give out a higher vibration. Begin with the opaque crystal and move on to the clear and golden when your energies have adjusted.

Azeztulite

Lemurian (trigonal; clear white, smoky, pink, golden, green, blue) Excellent for karmic and chakra cleansing, it opens new channels in the subtle and physical bodies. Assists in remembering our spiritual selves with All That Is. Grid for angelic contact, energy portals and regaining inherent abilities.

Lemurian

Paraiba Tourmaline (trigonal; turquoise) A new find, Paraiba is an enhanced Tourmaline with radiant heart energy that connects to the angels of truth and wisdom. Carries infinite compassion and encourages service to the planet and humanity. Calms over-reactions of the immune system and auto-immune diseases.

Paraiba Tourmaline

Moldavite

Moldavite (noncrystalline meteorite; deep olive green) Offers awareness of cause and source of dis-ease and supports healing, identifying the gift within illness and potentials. Aligns the chakras, integrates the divine blueprint, and accelerates spiritual growth. Brings you into communication with your higher self and cosmic messengers.

Phenacite

Phenacite (trigonal; white, clear, pink) Purifies and raises consciousness to a high frequency, bringing cosmic information to earth. It heals the soul and prepares subtle and physical bodies as a vehicle for the activated lightbody. Energies are available to those who have shifted their personal vibration to a higher level. Amplifies the energy of other healing crystals.

Spirit Quartz

Spirit Quartz (trigonal; white, smoky, "citrine") Provides insights into family problems, tightly focusing healing that reaches multidimensions. It promotes self-forgiveness and reprogrammes cellular memory. Spirit Quartz takes you to meet the spirits of your ancestors and can be programmed for ancestral healing, and reframing the past. An excellent stone to accompany the dying.

Selenite (monoclinic; white) Existing at the interface between spirit and matter, Selenite is crystallized divine light and anchors the lightbody in incarnation. Helpful for ascertaining your soul purpose and when you are still working on lessons. It is water soluble.

Polished Selenite

Petalite (monoclinic; white, pink) Assisting in spiritual purification and ancestral healing, Petalite is a shamanic crystal. Ideal for guiding a vision quest and for aligning the aura and opening the higher crown chakras.

Petalite

Tugtupite (tetragonal; pink, white, gray) Although exceedingly rare and expensive, Tugtupite is one of the most valuable crystals for heart-healing and awakening the heart-seed chakra (below the breastbone). It unites a compassionate heart with an illumined mind, bringing infinite peace. Useful for defending your liver against other people's anger. It promotes forgiveness and the ability to give of oneself in service.

Tugtupite

Satyamani Quartz

Satyamani/Satyaloka Quartz (trigonal; clear, white, yellow, gray) Prepared by monks in the Himalayas to bring the flame of pure consciousness to earth and to facilitate a vibrational shift in healing, they infuse the body with transformational energy. When placed on the soma chakra they activate the light- body and on the third eye the illumined mind. Combines well with Nirvana Quartz .

Purple Nirvana Quartz

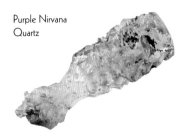

Nirvana Quartz (trigonal; white, pink, purple) Another of the Himalayan Quartzes, Nirvana Quartz is a crystal for spiritual alchemy and enlightenment. It holds crystallized divine consciousness and facilitates a profound shift in awareness, helping the soul to shed its karmic load. Excellent for opening the soul star chakra.

Blue Moonstone

Blue Moonstone (monoclinic; blue on white) One of the most powerfully activating stones for unawakened spiritual potential, Blue Moonstone prepares the physical body for the incorporation of the lightbody and reaches extremely high levels of consciousness. Place on the back of the neck to release muscle tension and allow subtle energies to flow through this area.

Crystal rituals and journeys

Rituals are a way of drawing something into your life. Whether you require abundance, assistance, or love, all you need do is choose the right crystals and carry out the rituals respectfully with focused attention and intention. Journeys offer another powerful way to work with crystals, and this chapter's exercises end with a journey into the unconditional love and acceptance of All That Is (see pages 336–38).

Although undertaking a ritual or journey is a serious matter that demands focus and intention, rituals and journeys also take you into a bright and joyful, almost playful, connection with your crystal companions. It is as if the crystal enjoys the experience as much as you do.

Timing rituals

Planning the timing can make an immense difference to the success of a ritual. If you want to draw something into your life, perform your ritual under the light of the new moon and continue until full moon, and if you want to send something out into the world, perform it at full moon time and continue until new moon.

Preparing the room

Rituals are best carried out in a prepared space (see pages 124–28). It is also traditional to bathe and put on clean clothes before performing a ritual and to work in candlelight. If you are journeying or carrying out a ritual or journey, make sure that phones are turned off and you will not be disturbed.

Amethyst geode

Attracting love

Crystals are just waiting to bring more love into your life, and nothing is more effective at attracting love than Rose Quartz. Place a big chunk of this beautiful crystal, activated to bring an abundance of love, in the relationship corner of your home (the far right corner from the door). Alternatively, place it by your bed, asking it to attract exactly the right partner for you—you won't have to wait long! Indeed, one woman found the effect so powerful that she had to cool it down with a gentle Amethyst to bring in one potential lover at a time and to enable her to choose the right man.

Using affirmations

Making an affirmation while holding a crystal is a powerful ritual in itself that takes only a few moments of your time. This ritual requires total focus and intention while you carry it out, and the more emotion you can put into an affirmation, the stronger it will be. To make a love affirmation, for example, hold a piece of Rose Quartz or Danburite and repeat the following words several times a day. It is important that you phrase the affirmation in the present tense to bring it into manifestation—"I attract love into my life, my life is full of love right now, my life is full of abundant love, I am a magnet for love"—and then let it go.

Rose Quartz

Attracting love

Carrying out rituals with crystals to attract or re-energize love can be highly potent. The love ritual on pages 232–33 uses romantic Rose Quartz, which is surprisingly powerful for such a gentle crystal. This becomes less surprising perhaps when you learn that pink—and Rose Quartz—is associated with Venus, the goddess of love and desire. Amorous Venus rules passion and eroticism, love and affection, and so Rose Quartz attracts a love that is tender and passionate, erotic and exciting. Adding Danburite to Rose Quartz emphasizes the unconditional, mutually supportive twin-flame aspect of love. This crystal packs a powerful punch into a small space. If you desire loving, supportive companionship, you could replace the Danburite with Sugilite. And if it's a hot date you are after, replace Danburite with lusty Ruby or fiery Garnet, powerful attractors of erotic love. Green Aventurine invites passion into the lives of those of more mature years.

When you are intending to perform a love ritual, try wearing pink or red, depending on whether you want to attract romance or red-hot passion. If you wish, you can also burn a sweetgrass smudge or rose incense to prepare the room, and anoint yourself with rose oil. Pink candles will set the scene and the right background music will assist your concentration—try playing Track 3 on the CD. When you are carrying out a love ritual, consciously make your movements slow and sensuous and move with voluptuous intent.

With imagination and the right stones you can adapt the love ritual on page 232–33 for other purposes: for an abundance ritual, use Grossular Garnet, Citrine, Carnelian, Green Aventurine, in a Star of David grid (see page 128); to call in assistance, use Selenite, Celestite, or any of the angelic-attuned stones; and to connect to All That Is, use an Amethyst or other crystal geode.

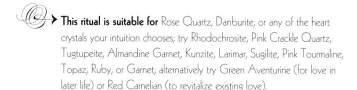

This ritual is suitable for Rose Quartz, Danburite, or any of the heart crystals your intuition chooses; try Rhodochrosite, Pink Crackle Quartz, Tugtupeite, Almandine Garnet, Kunzite, Larimar, Sugilite, Pink Tourmaline, Topaz, Ruby, or Garnet; alternatively try Green Aventurine (for love in later life) or Red Carnelian (to revitalize existing love).

Work with your crystals now Use your intuition to choose a suitable crystal (see pages 20–21), then for a ritual to attract love into your life turn to Exercise 29: My Attracting Love Ritual on pages 232–33, or for a journey to connect with All That Is, turn to Exercise 30: My Wholeness Meditation on pages 236–37.

I'm not quite there yet Ask yourself why you are not ready to call love into your life. You may have a perfectly valid reason that makes this ritual inappropriate at this time or you may need to do more work on self-development to open your heart to receive love (see pages 218–20).

EXERCISES TO TAKE CRYSTAL WORK FURTHER

These exercises will help you to attune to higher vibration crystals and to carry out rituals or journeys and meditations. They will increase your capacity to attract and give out love and to connect with All That Is in harmony with your crystal companions.

Exploring high-vibration crystals

Practice this exercise to feel the difference between higher and lower vibration crystals. It is suitable for use with crystals such as an ordinary clear Quartz point and one of the high-vibration Quartzes such as a Brandenberg, or with an ordinary Moonstone and a Rainbow or Blue Moonstone (which have progressively higher frequencies). Some of the higher vibration crystals are a more refined form of a crystal that already has a high vibration: Spectrolite is a higher resonance of Labradorite, for instance, although Labradorite is itself a high-vibration crystal.

 Exercise 27 COMPARING MY HIGH- AND LOW-VIBRATION CRYSTALS
CD REFERENCE TRACK 3 (OPTIONAL)

- **You will need**: pairs of cleansed and activated higher and lower vibration crystals (see above)

- **Place the pairs of crystals** on a table in front of you, well spaced out. Put your receptive hand first over the lower vibration crystal and attune to its energy.

- **Now put your receptive hand over** the higher vibration crystal until you can attune to its energy. Notice the difference between the two crystals and how this one affects your body and the subtle energy field around you. Note whether this crystal takes you to a higher dimension or opens a higher chakra.

- **Repeat the exercise** with another pair of crystals. Do this until you have worked with each of the pairs. Try changing hands to feel the difference.

My high- and low-vibration crystal experience

Date _____ Time _____

Pair of crystals _____

My experience _____

_____

What I noticed about the lower vibration crystal _____

_____

What I noticed about the higher vibration crystal _____

_____

Date _____ Time _____

Pair of crystals _____

My experience _____

_____

What I noticed about the lower vibration crystal _____

_____

What I noticed about the higher vibration crystal _____

_____

Working with high-vibration crystals

Not every high-vibration crystal will resonate with you, and the key to succesful working with crystals is to find the ones to which you can attune. If the crystal provokes a healing challenge, remove it and hold a Smoky or Chlorite Quartz between your feet to stabilize your energies. Return to the crystal when you have completed your healing or choose another.

 Exercise 28 ATTUNING TO MY HIGH-VIBRATION CRYSTALS CD REFERENCE

TRACK 2 (TO FOLLOW THE SCRIPT, TURN TO PAGES 244–45)

- **You will need:** various cleansed and activated high-vibration crystals (see the High-vibration Crystal Directory on pages 212–17)

- **Hold a high-vibration crystal gently** and sit quietly listening to track 2 on the CD. Your body may vibrate as it attunes to the crystal or you may be instantly transported to another energetic dimension; both reactions show that this crystal will work with you. If this does not happen, choose another crystal to work with, and try this one later when your vibrations have shifted.

- **Once you have established contact** with a crystal, lie down and place it on your higher chakras (see pages 92–93) to see what effect that has. If appropriate, allow the crystal to open these chakras. Ask the crystal to introduce its energetic capabilities to you and to show you how to work with it for best results. Remember to record any additional properties you discover about the crystal.

- **Repeat the exercise** with another high-vibration crystal when appropriate. Don't forget to record your observations in the space provided.

My high-vibration attuning experience

Date _____ Time _____

Crystal _____

My experience _____

_____

_____

_____

_____

_____

Date _____ Time _____

Crystal _____

My experience _____

_____

_____

_____

_____

_____

Date _____ Time _____

Crystal _____

My experience _____

_____

_____

_____

_____

_____

_____

_____

Date _____ Time _____

Crystal _____

My experience _____

_____

_____

_____

_____

_____

_____

_____

Date _____ Time _____

Crystal _____

My experience _____

_____

_____

_____

_____

_____

_____

_____

Date _____ Time _____

Crystal _____

My experience _____

_____

_____

_____

_____

_____

_____

_____

Calling-in love ceremony

This attracting love ritual is a powerful one; do it with unconditional love and compassion for yourself and with the intention of attracting toward you the most perfect love imaginable. If you already have a lover, rather than calling in your twin-flame in the ritual, ask that more love manifests between you and your lover and that the relationship becomes the best it can possibly be. The most potent time to practice this ritual is at the new moon.

 ## Exercise 29 MY ATTRACTING LOVE RITUAL
CD REFERENCE TRACK 3 (OPTIONAL)

- **You will need**: 4 cleansed and activated Rose Quartz and Danburite crystals, 4 pink candles in 4 Rose Quartz holders, silk cloth

- **Place the crystals and candles** on a table covered with the silk cloth. Position one candle to the north, welcoming in love from that direction as you light it. Place the others to the south, east, and west, again welcoming love from each direction as you light the candles.

- **Take your Rose Quartz crystals** into your hands and sit facing the table (if the crystals are large, hold one at a time or place your hands over them). Close your eyes and quietly attune to the crystals.

- **Let the energy of the crystals flow** through your hands, up your arms, and into your heart. As the energy reaches your heart, feel it open out and expand. Touch the crystals to your heart. Rose Quartz is a powerful heart cleanser and healer, so allow your heart to be purified by the energies of the crystals. Say, out loud: "I am a magnet for love. I welcome love into my heart and love into my life." Place the crystals back on the table in the appropriate place.

- **Pick up the Danburite**. Say out loud, "I call on my twin-flame to be present and to manifest fully and lovingly in my life" or, "I call on the love between my lover and myself to manifest fully and unconditionally, loving and supporting us both."

- **Sit quietly for a few moments** with your eyes focused on the crystals. Picture how life will be when you have the deeply passionate and mutually supportive love of your twin-flame at your side, or when you and your lover manifest all the love that is possible between you. Send that picture out into the future, unrolling it before you so that you walk that path with love.

- **When you are ready** to complete the ritual, get up and blow out each candle in turn saying: "I send light and love into the world and it returns to me tenfold." Either leave the crystals on the table or place them around your bed. Don't forget to record your experience in the space provided.

My attracting love experience

Date _____   Time _____

Crystals _____
_____
_____

My experience _____
_____
_____
_____
_____
_____
_____
_____
_____
_____
_____
_____
_____
_____
_____
_____
_____

The result of my experience _____

_____

_____

_____

_____

_____

_____

_____

_____

Was anything standing in the way of me accepting love? _____

_____

_____

_____

_____

_____

_____

_____

_____

_____

_____

Connecting to All That Is

This is one of my favorite meditations. I have practiced it for more than 35 years and never tire of it. The cave always expands and takes me to a new part of myself and All That Is. Give yourself plenty of time to practice this exercise and make sure that you will not be disturbed. If you have a big Amethyst geode that is too large for you to hold, place it on a table in front of you. You can expand on the exercise on future occasions by checking out whether there are any areas of the cave you have not visited, especially at the higher levels. Look out for hidden doorways and narrow tunnels. Explore whatever you find there, asking for a light to show you the way.

Exercise 30 MY WHOLENESS MEDITATION
CD REFERENCE TRACK 3 (OPTIONAL)

- **You will need**: a cleansed and activated Amethyst geode (see page 218).

- **Sit comfortably and look carefully** at your Amethyst geode. When you can remember its contours, close your eyes. Without opening your eyes, look up to the point above and between your eyebrows, your "third eye." Feel this eye open. Breathe gently and withdraw your attention from the outside world, focusing it deep inside yourself.

- **Hold your Amethyst** in whichever hand feels comfortable or place your hands on it and be aware of its vibrations radiating up your arm and into your third eye at the center of your forehead; feel its energy opening and expanding your inner awareness.

- **Now picture yourself standing** on the bank of a wide river that is flowing gently to the sea. Upstream in the far distance you can see high blue mountains and, at their foot, a shining lake. In front of you is a small wooden jetty with a boat tied up beside it. A boatman is waiting to help you into the boat.

- **Settle yourself comfortably** in the boat and visualize the boatman casting the boat off and guiding it upstream, moving quickly against the current. You can see the banks passing by and soon the river opens out into a beautiful lake. As you cross the lake, you can see a narrow river is coming down from the mountains and flowing into the lake. The boatman takes you as far up this river as it is possible to go. He ties up the boat and helps you out onto a rocky ledge.

- **Follow this ledge up into the mountains**; as it twists and turns you can see light shining in front of you until you enter a crystal cave. The cave is a huge Amethyst geode, light flickering from its every point.

- **Find a comfortable place to settle yourself** and allow yourself to merge with the energy of the Amethyst, enfolded within the geode. Let your spirit become one with the infinity of being. Ask the Amethyst to show you your soul path.

- **When you have found your soul path**, ask to be shown the guides and helpers who surround you in the unseen world. Ask them how they can help you and set out any specific requests you have for assistance.

- **Now let your spirit become one** with the infinity of being. Become aware of how ancient the crystal is, how it is light personified and how it is the divine taking on form. Then let your spirit become one with the infinity of being. Let go. Expand into All That Is. Simply merge and be.

- **When you are ready to leave** the crystal cave, withdraw into yourself once more, but retain your connection to the whole through the Amethyst in your hand.

- **Make your way back down the ledge** to where the boatman waits for you. Settle yourself in the boat and allow him to quickly propel the boat back down the narrow river and across the wide shining lake. In front of you, see the point you set out from; soon the boat is tying up at the bank. Thank your boatman for the journey and make your way back onto the bank.

- **When you have finished the journey**, thank the crystal for its light and your guides and helpers for their assistance and ask that they be always with you.

- **Let the light crystallize** at the outer edges of your aura, protecting you within a bubble of light. Take your attention down to your feet. Become very aware of the contact they make with the earth. Feel them holding you and grounding you on the earth and into your body. Then, when you are ready, open your eyes. Don't forget to record your experience in the space provided.

My Amethyst wholeness meditation experience

Date _____ **Time** _____

My experience _____

_____

How easily did I surrender to the boatman guiding the journey? _____

_____

Was the river straight or winding? _____

_____

Was I content to go with the flow or did I push against the river? _____

_____

What is my soul path? _____

_____

How did it feel to be part of the infinity of being? _____

_____

How did it feel to simply be and go with the flow? _____

_____

How can I incorporate that beingness into my everyday life? _____

_____

Was it possible to bring back my connection with the greater whole? _____

_____

How can I maintain the interface between me and the rest of the world? _____

_____

How did it feel to withdraw back into myself? _____

_____

Are there parts of myself that are uncommitted to the journey? _____

_____

Who are my guides and helpers? _____

_____

What do they do for me? _____

_____

Is this still appropriate? _____

_____

Do I need to renegotiate any agreements I made with them? _____

_____

How can they best assist me on my soul path? _____

_____

What other dimensions did I discover to the cave? _____

_____

INSPIRATIONS

You will find these meditations and journeys together with
a music-only track on the CD that accompanies this book.
Use them as directed in the exercises or let them inspire
your own journeys.

Relaxation, focusing, and opening the mind's eye

THIS TRACK HELPS YOU TO RELAX, FOCUS, AND OPEN YOUR MIND'S EYE

- **Settle yourself in a comfortable place** where you will not be disturbed. Breathe gently and easily, focusing on your breath for 10 breaths. As you breathe out, let go any tension you may be feeling. Pause. And then breathe in a sense of quiet peace.

- **Slowly raise and lower your eyelids** ten times, allowing your eyes to remain closed as you reach the tenth time. Your eyelids feel relaxed and pleasantly heavy. Keeping your eyes closed, raise your eyebrows high and stretch your whole face. Relax and let go. Let the relaxed feeling from your eyelids travel slowly up your forehead and across your scalp, and through all your facial muscles. Smile as widely as you can, move your jaw from side to side, and allow your face to relax.

- **Now lift your shoulders up to your ears** and let go. Allow the relaxed feeling to flow on down through your body. Take a big breath and sigh out any tension you may be feeling. Let your chest and back relax and soften.

- **Clench your fists and let them relax** on your thighs. Allow the sense of relaxation that is passing through your body to go down your arms. Any tension that is left drips out of your fingertips and trickles down to the earth.

- **Pull your belly in, breathing deeply.** Let all your breath out and count to 10. Allow your lower back and abdomen to feel warm and relaxed.

- **Let the feeling of relaxation go** on down through your thighs and knees, flowing down your legs to your feet. Raise and lower your feet and let your calf muscles be soft and loose. Scrunch your toes up and let them relax. If there is any tension left in your body, allow this to drain out of your feet.

- **You are now feeling comfortably warm** and peaceful, and yet receptive and alert. Spend a few moments enjoying this feeling of total relaxation. Notice how you remain mentally alert but physically relaxed.

- **Now gently focus your attention on your third eye**—the place between and slightly above your eyebrows. Without opening your eyes, look up to this space and sense, feel, or see an eye opening there. This is your inner eye, your mind's eye, through which you can use your intuition and focus your intention. This eye opens onto a screen on which you can see images when visualizing. The screen may be behind your third eye or out a foot or so in front of it. Remind yourself that at this moment your intention is to relax while remaining receptive, but that this intention changes, according to the exercise or journey you are undertaking in the future.

- **When you have finished your relaxation**, bring your attention back into your surroundings. Place your feet firmly on the floor and slowly sit up straight. Be aware of your connection with the earth. Get up and move around. If you feel the slightest bit floaty, hold Hematite or place your feet on a brown grounding crystal, such as Smoky Quartz, to connect you to the earth.

Attuning to my crystals

THIS TRACK HELPS YOU TO BRING YOUR ENERGIES INTO UNION
WITH THOSE OF A CRYSTAL

- **This track can be used** to get to know any crystal in your collection and to experience its energy. It talks you into a relaxed state, attunes you to the crystal, allows five minutes meditation time to be with the crystal, and then brings you out of the meditation again. Remember that crystal energy is subtle and it may take a little while for you to attune to the vibrations. Learning to recognize how you personally experience crystal energy is an essential first step.

- **Sit quietly holding your cleansed and dedicated crystal.** Breathe gently and allow yourself to relax and focus your attention on the crystal. State your intention to get to know this crystal a little better and to feel its energy.

- **Allow your eyes to go into soft focus** and gaze at the crystal. Note its shape, its color and size. Follow its contours and craters, if it has a "window" look inside. Feel how light or heavy the crystal is in your hand. Feel its vibrations and energetic resonance. You may feel your energy jump or tingle—like getting an electric shock —or slow and pulse as it connects to the crystal's energy. Allow the energy of the crystal to travel up your arms and into your heart and mind so that it reveals itself to you.

- **Be aware if the crystal** makes a special contact with any part of your body. If you wish, guide the energy up through your chakras and see if there is an energetic response.

- **If the crystal is transparent or translucent** allow your gaze to pass through the outer edge and into the center; follow the planes and landscape you find there.

- **When you are ready**, put your crystal down and consciously break off contact with its energies. Open your eyes fully and bring your attention into the room. Take your attention down to your feet and feel the contact they make with the floor. Feel your sit bones make contact with the chair and feel them supporting the weight of your body. Picture a bubble of protection all around you.

- **When you are ready**, stand up and move around, and record your insights.

The Quartz crystal journey

THIS TRACK HELPS YOU TO EXPERIENCE YOUR UNIQUE SENSE OF SELF AND HARNESS WAYS TO EXPRESS YOUR INDIVIDUALITY .

- **Sit comfortably and close your eyes.** Without opening your eyes, look up to the point above and between your eyebrows—your "third eye." Feel this eye open. Breathe gently and withdraw your attention from the outside world, focusing it deep inside yourself. Hold your Quartz crystal in whichever hand feels comfortable and be aware of its invigorating energy radiating out from the crystal and enfolding you. Feel how it enlivens every cell in your body, energizing and harmonizing as it goes.

- **Let the crystal take you deep down** into the part of you that is independent, individual, separate, and personal. Let it show you your ego—the part of you that has desires and drives. This is the place of your will, assertion, and aggression. Look carefully at what you are aiming for, what propels you to act as you do. And then look at what holds you back, how and where you procrastinate. Is there anywhere in your life where you always believe you are right no matter what anyone else says? Look, too, at where you are too self-absorbed or selfish to notice other people and their needs.

- **Then let the crystal move you** into the higher part of your being, your own unique Self, the divine part of your being that is housed at the core of your soul. Explore that Self.

- **Let the crystal take you deep down** to its base. Let it show you how it felt when it was part of a larger cluster, when it was part of the whole and connected to everything around it. Move your awareness out so that you too become part of the whole, and then withdraw it back into the birthing of your own unique Self. Find the point of balance between the two.

- **Let the crystal take you deep down** into your Self and connect you to the wisdom of the ages. Ask your Self to examine your shadow qualities with you and to show you what gift lies in the heart of each one and what energy you can reclaim from that shadow that will be useful in your life now.

- **Now feel yourself walking** with that Self, walking your pathway out into the future. As you travel that path, leave gifts for yourself that you will be able to pick up on your life's journey to enable you to express more of your unique Self and fulfill your potential.

- **When you have finished the journey,** bring your attention back into the present moment and picture light crystallizing at the outer edges of your aura, protecting you within a bubble of light.

- **Bring your hand down into your lap** and thank the crystal for its light. Detach from the crystal and put it aside.

- **Take your attention down to your feet.** Be very aware of the contact they make with the earth. Feel them holding you and grounding you on the earth and into your body. Then, when you are ready, open your eyes.

The Rainbow Obsidian journey

THIS TRACK HELPS YOU TO LET GO OF THINGS THAT ARE DETRIMENTAL TO YOUR CURRENT WELL-BEING AND RECOGNIZE YOUR INNER STRENGTHS

- **Settle yourself quietly** and breathe gently, withdrawing your attention from the outside world and into the crystal. Keep your eyes half-open and gaze at the bands of your Rainbow Obsidian. Move the crystal slightly so that it catches the best light to show you the coruscating bands. Feel the strength of the crystal in your hand. Let its energy radiate up your arms and into your heart. As you focus on each band let it take you inward. Allow the bands to move you gently into contact with your deepest Self. When you feel ready, place the crystal over your heart.

- **Ask the crystal** to let you know what you are holding onto; what it would be beneficial to release. Let it show you any hooks that are in your heart and gently dissolve these, filling the place with fresh energy and forgiveness. Ask the crystal to show you how your past is affecting your present in any area of your life.

- **Then willingly surrender all** that no longer serves you—all the pain and emotions, situations and experiences that have weighed you down and held you back. Acknowledge them and let them be drawn into the crystal for transmutation. Let them go with forgiveness in your heart.

- **Now ask the crystal** to show you the hidden gifts that lay hidden behind that old pain—the qualities you developed and the resources you can draw on. Allow yourself to know how you will use this.

- **Ask the crystal** if it has any other information for you and wait quietly for the answer.

- **Before you begin the return journey** put your attention out to the subtle bodies around your physical body and ask the crystal to draw off and transmute any negative energies or disharmonies, bringing all the subtle bodies into alignment. Then let the crystal draw off and transmute any negative energy, stress, or dis-ease in your physical body.

- **Now feel the strong protection** from the crystal that wraps around you in layers.

- **Finally, feel the strength of the crystal** and its powerful connection to the earth grounding and rooting you into your physical existence, bringing you fully into the present moment. When you feel ready, thank the crystal, open your eyes and move around.

Index

C

D

Acknowledgments

I would like to thank all the participants on my workshops who have helped to shape how I work with crystals. I have learned much from you all, and from all the crystal suppliers who introduce me to new crystals as they arrive. Finally, as always, thanks to David Eastoe (www.petaltone.co.uk) without whose cleansing essences I could not work.

Executive Editor: Sandra Rigby

Editor: Ruth Wiseall

Deputy Creative Director: Karen Sawyer

Designer: Cobalt

Assistant Production Controller: Vera Janke

Picture Research: Marian Sumega

Picture credits: Alamy Image Source Black 1. **Fotolia** aarnet 89. **Octopus Publishing Group** 2, 4, 6, 9, 10, 16, 17, 19, 23, 26, 27, 28, 29, 30, 31, 32, 49, 51, 53, 55, 56, 57, 58, 59, 60, 61, 63, 64, 81, 93, 113, 115, 117, 119, 122, 123, 124, 145, 150, 155, 156, 157, 159, 177, 179, 180, 182, 183, 185, 186, 209, 211, 212, 213, 216, 217, 218, 220, 223; /Andy Komorowski 21; /Frazer Cunningham 146; /Mike Prior 25, 83, 120, 125, 148; /Russell Sadur 13, 14, 91, 181, 191, 192, 219, 221